Six
Months
Off

HOPE DLUGOZIMA,
JAMES SCOTT, and DAVID SHARP

Six Months Off

*How to Plan,
Negotiate, and
Take the Break
You Need Without
Burning Bridges
or Going Broke*

An Owl Book
HENRY HOLT AND COMPANY
NEW YORK

Henry Holt and Company, Inc.
Publishers since 1866
115 West 18th Street
New York, New York 10011

Henry Holt® is a registered
trademark of Henry Holt and Company, Inc.

Library of Congress Cataloging-in-Publication Data
Dlugozima, Hope.
Six months off : how to plan, negotiate, and take
the break you need without burning bridges or going broke /
Hope Dlugozima, James Scott, and David Sharp.
p.   cm.
"An Owl book."
Includes index.
1. Leave of absence.   2. Sabbatical leave.   I. Scott, James
(James Donald, 1952–   . II. Sharp, David, 1958–   . III. Title.
HD5255.D58   1996   95-37728
331.25'763—dc20   CIP

ISBN 0-8050-3745-4

Henry Holt books are available for special
promotions and premiums.
For details contact: Director, Special Markets.

First Edition—1996

Designed by Victoria Hartman

Printed in the United States of America
All first editions are printed on acid-free paper.∞

10 9 8 7 6 5 4 3 2 1

To Tom. A very dear husband.
And a very dear friend.
—H.D.

To my wife, Mary. And to our sons,
Christopher and Alec.
—J.S.

To Sheila, who makes life
an unending sabbatical.
—D.S.

"I'm going to take a holiday for as long as I need."
"Just to play?"
"No! I want to find out why I'm working.
The answer can't just be to pay bills or to pile up
more money. . . . I can't find out sitting behind
some desk in an office. So, as soon as I get enough
money together, I'm going to knock off for a while.
Come back and work when I know what I'm
working for. Does that make sense?"

—*Cary Grant to Katharine Hepburn*
  in the 1938 movie Holiday

Contents

Acknowledgments

Finding the time to write a book about sabbaticals and the pursuit of leisure translates—ironically enough—into a lot of holidays and weekends spent at the computer. Joining us were a group of individuals who willingly gave us time out of their lives to help make *Six Months Off* a success. The authors wish to express their appreciation to the following people:

Our editor, Theresa Burns, for her invaluable editorial guidance and unflagging dedication to quality. She paid us the ultimate compliment by taking a sabbatical after we finished the book.

Our agents, Ling Lucas and Ed Vesneske, Jr., for ably navigating this project through the straits of publishing.

Our skilled and dedicated researchers: Sheila De La Rosa, Steven Finch, Mary Scott, and David Widner. Without their help, this book would still be a bundle of blank pages.

Those who believed in this book and supported it from the beginning: Owen Edwards, Cynthia Gorney, Katy Hall, Susan Margolis, James Morgan, and Catharine Norton.

Those who generously contributed their time and expertise: Cornelius Bull, the president of the Center for Interim

Programs, who offered wonderful insights into the sabbatical business and even sent one of us on an escape of her own; Kathleen Tucker, the host of the America Online's Travel Forum and a one-woman encyclopedia of useful travel tips, who gave us both ideas on where to search for more information and the on-line names of other sabbatical takers; Portland, Oregon–based career consultant Marti Chaney, who was a gold mine of wisdom on matters work related; Martha Peak, group editor at the American Management Association, who steered us to important contacts and whose keen managerial insights were reflected in the textbook-perfect quality of her own sabbatical; Patricia Long, a staff writer at *Health* magazine, who reviewed an early draft of the book and offered many helpful suggestions on how to make it even better; and Teo Furtado, who helped us turn a vague idea into a *book*.

Finally, the hundreds of people who shared their sabbatical stories with us. Thank you for teaching us the true value of time.

Six Months Off

Introduction

IT'S ABOUT TIME

Imagine a great gulp of time that is all your own. Six months, say, to get reacquainted with your friends and family, to travel, to *finally* finish the renovations on your house. Six months to learn a new language or a new technology. Six months to do good in the world—or do nothing.

Just think of it. Off to school to study computer graphics or fabric design or Mediterranean cooking. Off to Argentina to work on a cattle ranch. Off to New Orleans to play the sax in small jazz clubs until two in the morning—or to Southern California to study filmmaking. Off to Budapest to become editor of an English-language weekly. Off to Ireland to read a stack of books taller than you in a cottage overlooking Dingle Bay. Off across the country in an RV, with your spouse and kids in tow, all of you talking again. Off to the coast of Maine to learn how to build your own house. Off to Canada to hike the entire coastline of Newfoundland.

It's quite a fantasy, isn't it? And not just any fantasy, it turns out. Taking a long break from the daily grind now ranks right up there with winning the lottery as among the most widely and deeply held of the American daydreams.

According to a national poll conducted by Bruskin and Associates, almost seven in ten people who make $40,000 or more a year fantasize about taking at least several months off, and one in five 35- to 49-year-olds fantasizes about it *daily.*

We can't help ourselves. We're a generation, after all, who grew up with summer vacations; the idea that we should have a few months off every so often to renew ourselves is wired into our collective memories. We hear about a co-worker taking a few months off to go on an archaeological dig in Wyoming or a family down the street taking a year off to live in Costa Rica, and our world opens up, bright with possibilities. Surely, we think, there must be a way to do what they did, to take an occasional break without jeopardizing everything we've spent years building: Our homes and families. Our careers and savings. Our futures.

But how?

Four years ago, when the three of us began to explore the idea of writing a book about taking an occasional break from the rat race, the need was already painfully clear. Now that need is well past the breaking point. Spurred by an increasingly competitive global economy, we're putting in so many extra hours at work these days that "free time" sounds like an oxymoron. We call clients on the cellular phone during the morning commute, work furiously during long business flights, carry notebook computers and modems and portable fax machines so that we're never more than an arm's length away from the office.

Already we work more hours than anyone in Europe. We outwork the industrious Germans, for instance, by the equivalent of more than three weeks a year. We work longer hours than our parents did by the equivalent of an extra month a year. In the United States today, one employed person in four puts in at least forty-nine hours at work each week; one in eight works sixty hours or more. Only the Japanese, who are literally dying of overwork in such numbers that they've created a word for the phenomenon, *karoshi*, put in more hours.

The picture looks even worse when you look at a typical family. "Largely because more women have taken jobs outside the home," says Harvard economist Juliet Schor, author of *The Overworked American*, "a typical family is putting in a thousand more hours a year today than they were twenty-five years ago."

And what do we do in our so-called leisure hours? We run errands, balance the checkbook, cook dinner, mow the lawn, and do the laundry. Oh, yes, and feel guilty that we can't seem to find the time to stay in closer touch with friends and family, keep up with our reading, throw swell dinner parties, and volunteer at the local food bank—not to mention exercise.

Things have gotten so bad, social scientists tell us, that like overstressed lab rats, we have developed dysfunctional attitudes about time itself. We divide our days into nanoseconds, says Geoffrey Godbey, a professor of leisure studies at Penn State University, and attempt to cram more and more experiences into every waking moment. "We listen to music while we jog," he says. "We substitute quicker activities for slower ones." What's happening, Godbey says, is that we're trying to increase the yield on the decreasing amount of leisure time we have left. "Ten years ago, people went to the zoo for the whole day," he says. "They packed a lunch, the old man fell asleep on the grass, the kids cased the place, then took time to go back to the animals they were really interested in. Now a family jumps on the interstate, takes thirty-five minutes to drive through Animal Safari, and it's on to the next thing."

All that hustle and bustle might bring us material and even some psychic rewards, but it seldom adds up to a meaningful whole. The problem, says University of Chicago psychologist Mihaly Csikszentmihalyi, is that without enough time to reflect, we're not able to tie the increasing number of experiences in our lives together. Without those connections, he says, we feel pulled in too many directions at once. We can no longer make sense of the world; we feel chronically anxious.

The need for big chunks of time—to think, to recharge our emotional, creative, and spiritual batteries, to learn critical new skills, to simply gain the perspective necessary to make sense of a rapidly changing world—has never been greater. Time rejuvenates us, the experts say. It makes us better workers, better parents and spouses, better human beings. It broadens our bandwidth and reminds us who we are.

In these past few years, we've interviewed more than 200 people, from every imaginable occupation, including a submarine navigator, an advertising executive, a water-quality engineer, and a map buyer. Many of the people we talked to responded to a notice we posted on computer bulletin boards seeking people who had taken sabbaticals, or they answered a classified ad we placed in several newspapers. Others we found through professional and civic organizations. Still others we heard about through friends or coworkers. Once the word got out, it seems, we couldn't turn around without running into someone who had either taken a long leave or knew someone who had.

As might be expected, some of the people we interviewed were born risk takers. At some point in their careers, they had simply quit their jobs in frustration or exhaustion, hoping things would somehow work out at the other end. In most cases, it did, although not always without a few bumps. They simply got off the fast track and after a few months of bicycling through Europe or sitting around in their own living rooms, merged right back into the fast lane—more content and emotionally grounded than they'd been before they left but often poorer, as well.

But we also heard from a surprising number of people— most of them in their late twenties, thirties, and forties— who had planned their time off more carefully. These people, from social workers to marketing executives, journalists to high-powered attorneys, had been as smart about taking time off as they'd been about their work. Remarkably, many of these women and men had families, jobs they loved, *mortgages*. And yet they had found creative and effective ways to negotiate the time they needed, had chosen carefully how and where to spend their time, and then had planned a smooth and successful reentry to their old jobs—or even better jobs. Their stories resonated with, of all things, practical good sense.

A farm couple from Iowa, with 800 acres of land, two school-age daughters, and some sheep to worry about, went to Hungary for three months without spending a penny of their own money. Things went so smoothly that they're now thinking about taking a much longer leave—perhaps a year or more in Eastern Europe. A financial analyst for General Mills took two years off to join the Peace Corps and used the experience to win a plum assignment in Amsterdam. A psychologist received the blessings of his clients and employer to spend a year doing stand-up comedy by turning his passion into a research project. Others took time off for once-in-a-lifetime adventures. They hiked around Lake Superior, all 1,600 miles of it; bicycled across Siberia; climbed Africa's highest mountain, Mt. Kilimanjaro. Still others used a sabbatical to launch new careers. A computer programmer and amateur musician spent a year in Zimbabwe studying marimba music with that country's finest players. His twelve-month stay—in many ways, the equivalent of a master's degree—cost him about $2,000. A 41-year-old legal secretary talked her employer into four months off with half pay and full benefits so that she could take professional cooking classes. A Philadelphia investment manager and his fiancée spent a year traveling through Central America on his five-month severance check; afterward, they started their own business, a Spanish-language school that places Americans in private homes in Latin America.

Sure, some of the people we interviewed grumbled that they didn't get everything done they'd planned. Life can be so *real*, can't it? But, surprisingly, no one expressed regrets. They seemed content, to use an old-fashioned word, even exhilarated. The change itself, they said over and over, was good. Time away had given them a new perspective, confidence, a sense of achievement. Nearly everyone, if given the chance, said they would do it again.

They may just get the chance. Twenty years ago, sabbaticals were no more common than tenure anywhere outside of academia. Today, according to several national surveys, nearly two in ten American companies offer some kind of sabbatical, and more than seven in ten U.S. companies offer personal leaves of absence, which are often used for the same purpose. What's more, according to a recent survey by the International Foundation of Employee Benefit Plans, fully a third of American companies will begin offering sabbaticals within the next four years. Already, Federal Express, Du Pont, American Express, Nike, and many more big corporations have jumped on the sabbatical bandwagon, joining such longtime sabbatical givers as Time Inc., Xerox, Wells Fargo Bank, and McDonald's.

High-tech firms, such as Intel and Tandem Computers, have considered sabbaticals a necessity from the start. Even IBM and Apple Computer, despite their troubles in recent years, have stuck fast to what has become one of their employees' favorite benefits. Apple, for example, allows its employees to take six weeks off with full pay every five years—and many lengthen the time by tacking on vacation days or unpaid leave. IBM grants leaves with full benefits for up to three years, to be used for any "once-in-a-lifetime opportunity."

It's not just big businesses with deep pockets that are coming around, either. Restaurant workers, librarians, even doctors and attorneys are asking for and getting time off. Twenty years ago, when a partner at Denver's Holland & Hart complained that there had to be more to life than billable hours, the firm decided to give sabbaticals a try and began offering its busy partners three months off with full pay or six months off at half pay every five years. "We were skeptical at first about the cost, since law tends to be a very competitive business," says Bill McClearn, one of the partners. "Initially we adopted the program on a sunset basis; after five years, unless it was adopted by a supermajority of partners, it would simply lapse. But when the time came to vote, it was renewed by 100 percent of the partners. Nobody has questioned it since."

One reason, of course, for all this pro-sabbatical fervor is that more and more women are entering top-management ranks and bringing with them the idea that people are entitled to more balance in their lives. The Family Leave Act, passed in 1993, also has helped. Suddenly, every company in America with more than fifty employees has a reason—and a practical blueprint—to make a leave of absence work. After all, if a company must give its employees up to twelve weeks off to care for the birth or adoption of a child, aging relatives, or sick children as a matter of legal course, the company will begin to understand that it can offer extended leaves for other reasons, too—like letting a 40-year-old accountant take a few months off to renew his relationship with his school-age children. In short, employers will do it because they will know how to do it.

No, it's not altruism alone that's at work here. Most businesses, even those run by nice people with big hearts and social consciences to match, know they can't afford to slow the pace for everyone. But they also know they can't afford to burn out valued employees. The smart companies, the ones that have figured out that job satisfaction has a direct bearing on job performance, view sabbaticals as an investment in their most important resource: their employees. At San Francisco–based Genentech, for instance, company records show that employee departures, once widespread, dropped off significantly after the biotechnology giant established a generous sabbatical program.

Not everyone welcomes change, of course—or thinks that even an occasional break from the fast track is a good idea. When "Calvin and Hobbes" cartoonist Bill Waterson and *New York Times* columnist Anna Quindlen took sabbaticals several years ago to recharge their batteries, a lot of people warned them that they were putting their careers in jeopardy. When former Tennessee governor Lamar Alexander told his colleagues that he was planning to take six months off as soon as he left office to spend time with his family in Australia, then-Florida governor Bob Graham was even more direct. "You get off the political track," Alexander recalls him saying, "and you'll never get back on."

He went anyway, despite Graham's warning, and found it to be one of the most productive periods of his life. "I felt free, liberated," he says. "I'd take long walks. I read books that I hadn't read in thirty years, books I'd never have considered reading before. I would sit around and visit with my children, probably more than they'd like. As governor, there was so much output. I was always saying things to people, giving people instructions. I was riding a core of information and knowledge and attitudes that I'd collected a long time ago. And then for those six months away there was input. I was listening. I was sitting around, not running around. I was recharging. I was learning."

Alexander came back with not only a very different perspective but a renewed vigor for politics. After a short stint as the president of the University of Tennessee and another stint as Secretary of Education in the Bush administration, he got right back on perhaps the fastest track of all; in early 1995, he announced he was running for president of the United States.

Waterson, meanwhile, now virtually owns the comics page, and Quindlen has won a Pulitzer Prize for commentary and become a best-selling novelist.

We hope you'll get the message while reading this book that a sabbatical is a *practical* answer to the demanding, hurried pace of the 1990s. It's not so much an escape from work as it is a way to keep or put your life and career on track. In short, it's an investment. Six months off out of the 500 or more you'll probably work in the course of a lifetime can—with a little careful planning—make you more productive, happier in the long run.

How do you do that? How do you take time off and put it

to good use? The answer will be different for everyone, of course, but much of what you'll need to know can be found in the experiences of the people who have already successfully taken time off. Their insights and practical advice form the backbone of this book—and its most important lessons. *How to negotiate for the time you'll need. Where to find the money. How to effectively use the time you'll have. How to use a sabbatical to reenergize a stalled career or as a bridge to a new one. How to engineer a smooth reentry.* It's all here in gritty, honest detail.

Stick around. Time, after all, is on your side.

Overcoming the Big Buts

Just about everyone who thinks about taking a sabbatical eventually comes up against at least one big hurdle. Not enough money. Not enough time. A cranky boss. An unsupportive spouse or partner. Judy Garlan, the art director of *Atlantic Monthly* magazine and the mother of three-year-old twin boys, had an entirely different problem. It just never occurred to her that taking time off was an option.

Admittedly, Garlan had plenty of good reasons of her own not to consider it. Like most working mothers, she was too frazzled trying to make it through each day to spend a lot of time in deep thought. Her husband was already holding down two jobs: one as an editor for a trade magazine in New York City, which kept him away from their Boston home at least three days a week, and another as a freelance writer. She was putting in up to sixty hours a week at the office herself, often bringing work home with her, and doing her best to care for their two very active sons. She couldn't imagine squeezing so much as a two-week vacation into her busy schedule—much less a far lengthier break.

"At least once a month," says the 44-year-old Garlan, "I'd reach the point where I thought I couldn't handle it anymore.

I was getting the magazine out, but I wasn't taking care of the daily things. My husband would say, 'Quit your job.' But I love my work, and, frankly, I knew we couldn't afford it. We went round and round like that for a year until, finally, it occurred to me to ask myself what I really wanted. I figured, why not ask."

When Garlan sat down and took stock, she realized that she had been working for nearly twenty years without a break and her to-do list had simply got so long she could no longer keep up. There was just no time for things like getting the twins into nursery school, answering her mail, even learning the basic computer skills that were becoming increasingly important for her career. "Once I thought about it," she says, "I realized that what I really wanted was a long break. I knew that if I was going to do both my jobs well—at the magazine and at home—I needed a year just to catch up."

Garlan's timing couldn't have been better. Her boss, worried that he might lose one of the linchpins of his staff, embraced the idea. In fact, he not only agreed to the year off but volunteered to pay her benefits and a modest salary. Along with some savings and a small windfall her husband had just received from a writing project, it was enough to see them through the year. "My boss is a saint," she says. "I've been there almost fourteen years, and, luckily, he appreciates my work. He views this as insurance for the future." Garlan's husband also was pleased with her solution. "He told me, 'I'm surprised you didn't think of this before.' "

As we write, Garlan is four months into her year off and quickly making her way through an ambitious to-do list. She's sorting through their finances, organizing closets, buying long-needed bedroom furniture, hanging out at the playground with the other moms in the neighborhood, tend-ing to long-neglected friendships, and planning several family trips. She's even taking a computer class once a week and putting together form letters so that she'll have an easier time keeping up when she goes back to work. "Having this time is like being given oxygen," she says. "I feel this incredible relief."

Let's assume for a moment that you don't share Garlan's good fortune. Your boss isn't a saint; he's a grouch. And the significant others in your life aren't exactly supportive. What's more, unless Ed McMahon shows up on your doorstep with that long-promised $10 million check in his hand, you'd have trouble coming up with the cash for a long weekend at the Hyatt, much less, say, six months in Europe.

The good news is that you don't have to be anywhere near as lucky as Garlan to take time off. You don't even have to be especially resourceful, although, as you'll see, it helps. Below, we'll look at the four major hurdles that keep people stuck, preventing them from taking the break they need.

HURDLE #1: BUT I DON'T HAVE THE MONEY

There are four ways to come up with the money for a long break: (1) Win it. (2) Beg it. (3) Save it. (4) Or do without it. Sound flip? Let's take a look at each of these four strategies, one at a time.

Winning It: Grants, Scholarships, and Fellowships

Winning large amounts of cash—or prying it out of someone else's fingers—isn't as far-fetched as it sounds. According to

Dan Cassidy, president of the National Scholarship Research Service, foundations and corporations handed out more than $26 billion in 1994 in individual grants, scholarships, and fellowships. Another $2.9 billion went unclaimed, not because no one qualified but because no one bothered to apply.

An estimated 53,000 scholarships, grants, or fellowships, Cassidy says, are available for just the sorts of things most likely to attract someone contemplating a sabbatical. "There are funds earmarked for almost any purpose you can imagine," he says. "You can go on an archeological dig, take a cooking class in Paris, go off to study oceanography with Jacques Cousteau, even travel or write a book."

Cottages at Hedgebrook, for instance, a privately funded retreat on Whidbey Island in Washington State, each year provides more than a hundred women of all ages and abilities a fantasy come true: the chance to write whatever they want in peace and quiet while someone else tends to the cooking, the housekeeping, and the bills. Each woman is given free use of a luxuriously comfortable cottage for up to three months, hearty and healthful meals—lunch is actually brought to the door—and all the gorgeous scenery she can take in. Those who otherwise couldn't afford it are even given travel funds.

Best of all, unlike government-funded grants and scholarships, the application process itself for programs like Hedgebrook is relatively simple—and the money comes with few strings attached. There are generally no age or income restrictions, for instance, and it's perfectly acceptable to go after more than one grant or scholarship at a time if one won't cover all your expenses. "It's a lot easier than people think," says Cassidy. "There's something out there for almost everyone; you just have to find it."

Those searching for funds, Cassidy says, have three options. They can go to almost any large library and spend a few hours sorting through the big reference directories, buy or order the books at a bookstore, or use a research service like his. (See Resource Guide, page 229.) A database search is easy, but it's also pricey. You can expect to pay about $75 for a scholarship search and $350 for a search of the available grants and fellowships, Cassidy says.

Zeroing in on a big pot of fellowship gold isn't like winning the lottery. For starters, the odds are considerably better. At Hedgebrook, for instance, about 25 women out of about 200 applicants are chosen for each session. (See Chapter 3, page 67.) "Most people have a pretty good shot," Cassidy says. "Our studies show that about one in two people who make the effort get at least some money." The amount varies from about $500 to $60,000 or more, Cassidy says, and he estimates the average amount falls in the $10,000 to $15,000 range.

Grants and scholarships do have one thing in common with the lottery: you can't win if you don't play. When James Nelson first spotted an ad in the *Wall Street Journal* seeking applicants for the Eisenhower Exchange Fellowship, a program that sends Americans abroad to work with their counterparts in other countries, he didn't think he had a prayer's chance of being selected. One of a handful of attorneys working in the Mississippi Secretary of State's office, he applied on a lark anyway. "I envisioned all these Wall Street lawyers and big government officials applying," he says. "I thought my odds were pretty slim."

As it turned out, though, Nelson's experience in helping his state put some government-owned property back into private hands was just the sort of experience the selection committee was looking for. He was one of five people selected for the three-month fellowship.

"Once I stopped and thought about it, I could see a lot of similarities between conditions in Hungary and conditions in Mississippi," he says. "Both are rural, agricultural economies. And we were going through a lot of the same things. I was a better fit than I first thought."

Begging It: Getting Employers to Foot the Bill

Even if you don't qualify for a grant or scholarship, there's no reason you can't get someone to give you the money you'll need for your break. Surprisingly, even in the lean and mean nineties, many companies, along with churches, high schools and colleges, and other employers, offer sabbaticals as part of their basic benefits package. Many more, including those with only a handful of employees, offer at least partly paid leaves on a case-by-case basis.

Sometimes, as Judy Garlan found out, you just have to ask. Of course, as you'll learn in Chapter 4 about negotiation, your chances for success depend greatly on your relationship with your employer—and your own productivity. Let's be blunt. If an employer values you, you're much more likely to get what you're asking for. If you're not valued, you're probably not where you belong, anyway.

Suppose you work for someone who can't or won't fund your sabbatical. Or suppose, like nearly a third of American workers, you're either self-employed or work on a contract or temporary basis for one or more employers.

No matter. You still can get others to foot the bill. One option, for instance, is to work your way through an adventure. The Peace Corps, alone, has paid for more than 100,000 sabbaticals, and there are many similar options, from paid internships to other kinds of temporary work. If you're an accountant with a passion for rock and roll, for example, you might volunteer to crunch numbers for a particular band in exchange for the chance to go on tour with them. Or if you're a talented amateur photographer, you might talk a big film manufacturer into funding part or all of an intriguing photographic expedition.

With a little imagination, almost anything is possible. Doug Dawson, a self-employed Colorado artist, has talked his way into several paid sabbaticals around the world, including one that recently took him to tiny Suriname, in South America. After hearing about a group of translators who were trying to introduce the Bible in that country, it occurred to him that they might have better luck with a *slightly* different product. "The Bibles they were using had the old European illustrations," says Dawson, a devout Quaker. "As an artist, I thought it might be more appropriate to illustrate the text in images that reflected the lifestyle and dress of the peoples who would be seeing them."

Dawson, who loves to travel and was eager to brush up on his foreign-language skills, got in touch with the group and made them an appealing offer: if they would pick up most of his expenses for a long stay in South America, he would volunteer his time to illustrate the Bible for them.

It wasn't an immediate sale. But the group was intrigued enough to counter with an offer of their own. They wanted Dawson to teach several workshops in Suriname, so that local artists themselves could help with the illustrations. And they also wanted him to survey the four different indigenous peoples in the region to learn more about their tastes in book covers and typestyles. In the end, though, Dawson got his all-expenses-paid trip to South America and what turned out to be a rich and rewarding cultural experience, lasting nearly two months.

Saving It: The Reward Is Your Freedom

If a handout isn't in the cards, you can always get the money you need along more traditional lines. You might borrow from your life insurance policy or your 401(k) plan at work, for instance, or take out a home-equity loan. It makes sense if you're presented with a once-in-a-lifetime opportunity. But if you have the time, *save* the money you'll need instead. That way you won't limit your options when you get back.

"Planning for a sabbatical really comes down to one simple idea," says Marysue Wechsler, president of the Institute of Certified Financial Planners. "You have to be willing to live enough below your means today so that you can put money aside to do what you want *without* putting your future lifestyle at risk. Part of the answer might be that you can't take a sabbatical this year; you'll have to wait a few years. Or maybe you'll have to give up a few luxuries. But the sooner you start thinking and planning, the better."

The first step in that process, Wechsler says, is to sit down with two detailed budgets—one for the period of time you plan to be away and the other listing your current expenses. "You just go down the list of current expenses and see which can be transferred to the other column, which can't, and which can be cut altogether. Food, for example, can easily be transferred," she says. "But maybe the insurance on the house or car can't."

Most of us, it turns out, have more discretionary dollars in our pockets or bank accounts than we realize. In fact, surveys show that American households average at least $11,000 in discretionary income, money that goes toward such things as baseball tickets and designer shoes. Suppose, for example, that you're spending $50 every Friday night for dinner out. Total that up over the course of a year, and you'll find a quick $2,600 that could go toward your sabbatical.

Of course, it's far easier to save the money you'll need if you have a specific goal in mind. Thinking about spending a few months in Ireland? You'll find that giving up a night out isn't hard to do if you know that the money you're saving would pay for three nights' stay at a B&B in Dublin.

Doing Without: *The Minimum Expense Sabbatical*

One way to cut the cost of a sabbatical almost painlessly—and dramatically—is to simply lower your overhead during your break. If you rent, try to schedule your sabbatical so that it begins when your lease is up. Then put your worldly goods in storage for the duration of your time away. Or sublease your apartment, and save yourself the trouble of cleaning out your furniture and kitchen cupboards. If you own, consider renting out your house. Leave your furniture in place, and you can charge even more. Or swap houses with someone who lives where you want to spend your sabbatical. With at least a dozen house-swapping organizations available to help you do just that (see the Resource Guide), it's relatively easy to do. And you'll often have the advantage of being able to swap entire lifestyles—car, neighbors, the whole shebang, making your time away even more rewarding and affordable.

Cut everywhere you can. Pay off those credit cards. If you're leaving town, cancel your membership at the health club. Loan your car to a trustworthy friend, with the understanding that she'll make the payments while you're away. The idea is to get your monthly budget as close to zero as possible for the period you'll be away, so that every dollar you have available goes toward your sabbatical, not your old lifestyle.

Keep in mind that a sabbatical doesn't have to cost a small fortune. Spending a lot of money on four-star hotels or first-class travel, in fact, can often insulate you from the very experience you're looking for: an adventure. Just as important, think about how you can stretch the few dollars you have. Five thousand dollars, for instance, probably wouldn't see you through more than a month or two in Rome or San Francisco—especially if you check off more than one dependent on your tax return each year. But that same amount of money, in many parts of the world, would put you up in near luxury for a year.

The Third World may not be where you want to spend the rest of your life, says Rick Steves, author of *Europe Through the Back Door* and coauthor of *Asia Through the Back Door*, but it is greatly underrated as a destination for anyone who wants a dramatic and affordable change of scenery. "Many people who couldn't afford a short trip to Paris could sell their car and spend two years in places like Turkey or many parts of Asia," he says.

Even a more familiar destination like Portugal, he points out, offers just about everything a spoiled American could want: great people, great cuisine, great climate, and great prices. "I see a lot of expatriates and retired people there, and they are just so smug about it," Steves says. "They have the world by the tail."

Attorney Baine Kerr's family actually *saved* money during their year-long sabbatical in Costa Rica, even though he was getting paid just half his usual salary. How? They rented out their house in Boulder, Colorado, for $1,400 a month—$400 more than the rent they paid in Costa Rica, leaving them with enough left over to cover food and most other incidentals. For transportation, they bought a used Volkswagen van that took them everywhere and then resold it just before they returned home.

The Kerrs didn't take a vow of poverty during their stay. Three or four dollars a week bought the family of four all the fresh fruit, vegetables, and most other staples they could eat. Health care, available free through the government, was at least as good as they had back home. Their kids went to a terrific English-language school in San José, Costa Rica's capital city. And for recreation, they read, went horseback riding by moonlight in the 7,000-foot-high cloud forest of Monteverde, went camping or to the beach, or simply went for long walks around San José itself. The place they rented—within walking distance of the city center—was a big Latin-style, five-bedroom house built around a sunny patio.

"We could have gotten a place for much less," Baine Kerr says. "It was extravagant by Costa Rican standards, but that's where we decided to spend most of our money. You can live very comfortably on almost nothing," he adds, "if you're willing to give up a few luxuries."

Transport yourself, and you can save even more. If your goal, for instance, is simply to spend six months or more in the slow lane, why not do just that? Take a hike. Or paddle your way up the coast of Maine or Baja in a sea kayak. No form of transportation is cheaper than your own muscles. Each time you buy gasoline, purchase a bus ticket, or hop a plane, you shorten the length of time that you can afford to travel.

You might walk the entire 2,600-mile length of the Pacific Crest Trail from Mexico to Canada, for instance, for no more than a few thousand dollars, including what you'll spend on boots, tent, sleeping bag, and other equipment.

Not only will you experience a slower pace and traverse landscapes as beautiful as anything Ansel Adams ever pointed a camera at, but you'll walk away with some lasting benefits: stronger calves, a clear head, and the sense of accomplishment that comes from meeting an ambitious challenge.

Go by bicycle, and you'll cover even more territory, as well as see parts of the world where cars and buses just don't go. Deborah Harse, a 38-year-old masseuse from New York City, has seen much of the world in the past ten years from the seat of a bike—at a cost of about $10 a day. One five-month sabbatical took her to China, where, after pedaling across a vast stretch of Inner Mongolia, she happened on a group of children on horseback, herding sheep and singing at the top of their lungs. Other trips have taken her to Russia and Central America. Her most recent adventure took her to Cambodia and Vietnam for the second time.

How does she do it? She travels light, keeps shopping to a minimum, stays off the beaten tourist path, and takes advantage of organizations like Servas International, a worldwide network of travelers and host families whose goal is to promote world peace through brief homestays with people of different backgrounds. Servas members share meals and accommodations with host families; lodging is generally free. In Guatemala, she met a woman who ended up teaching her how to weave; Harse spent a month living with the woman and her family and has stayed in close touch with her since.

HURDLE #2: I CAN'T FIND THE TIME!

Giving employees time off isn't exactly virgin territory for most employers. After all, most companies routinely must deal with pregnancy leave, along with leaves for health problems and other personal matters. And just about every employer is at least grudgingly familiar with *vacations*. But let's say you can't imagine talking your employer into granting you six months off—or even three months off. Or maybe you don't work for a company at all; you work for yourself. What then?

Take a Break During a Natural Transition in Your Life

Today's topsy-turvy world of downscaling, outsizing, and rightsizing might be downright scary at times, but it also represents an opportunity. The upside to insecurity in the workplace is that unlike our parents' generation, we're *not* tied to one company for forty years. A break in employment is no longer necessarily seen as a negative thing.

One of the best times to take a break is when you're between jobs, between school and job, or simply at a career crossroads. Not only are those the times that naturally lend themselves to a period of self examination but they're also the most *convenient* for you and your employer.

That's exactly what Brian Booth did. After working for five years as a nuclear propulsion officer on a navy submarine, the 33-year-old Illinois native decided to change careers but wasn't ready to jump immediately into the corporate world—and for good reason. During his stint on board the submarine, he put in an average 100 hours a week on the job. "I figured I worked the equivalent of thirteen years on that ship, and I deserved a break," he says.

Taking advantage of the natural transition in his life, Booth asked the navy to ship his belongings to a storage facility, and he spent seven months hiking the Pacific Crest

Trail before settling into a job as an engineer with the Boeing company in Seattle. "Hiking the trail fit into my life just like a key fitting into a lock," he says.

Less dramatic transitions can also be a good time to take a break. If you're planning to move, for example, you might sell your house but delay moving into a new home until after your sabbatical. Similarly, you might extend a pregnancy leave or a long vacation into an even longer break.

Often, too, you can take advantage of subtle changes going on at work. One of the things that worked in Judy Garlan's favor when she asked for a year off was that the magazine she worked for was about to undergo a shift to computer-assisted design. One way or another, Garlan would have to bring in someone from the outside to help the magazine through the transition. By taking a leave at just that time and hiring a temporary art director with the technical skills and experience she lacked, she saved her employer the cost of hiring a lot of expensive consultants and made the transition easier for everyone involved.

Trade Income for Time

Whether you work for yourself or someone else, you make the same bargain: you trade your time and labor for money. But the reverse is also often possible: you can trade income or labor for time.

You might, for example, give up a bonus or a raise for extra time off. After all, it's always easier to give up money that's not in your hand than it is to give up cash that's already been earmarked for spending. Or you might volunteer to take an unpaid leave during a period when business is slack. By doing so, you could even end up saving your job. At the very least, you'll probably win the gratitude of a boss, eager to both hold on to valued employees and tend to the bottom line.

Du Pont offers full benefits for leaves taken during slow periods to help ease the ups and downs of business cycles. And Hallmark Cards, AT&T, and many other companies offer similar programs.

Another option is to volunteer for a special project. Say your employer wants to get a new widget on the market in a hurry but can't really afford to hire extra employees. By putting in lots of extra hours now, you can bargain for more time off later.

Christopher Darden, a lawyer for the Los Angeles district attorney's office, struck that very bargain when he agreed to join the team prosecuting O. J. Simpson. He had already accumulated more than 800 hours of comp time in the understaffed prosecutor's office at the time he was asked to join the team, and he knew there would be a lot of late nights during the trial. He agreed, with one stipulation: when it was all over, he'd take his time off in one big chunk.

Choose an Occupation That Has Built-In Opportunities for Taking Time Off

If you're thinking about switching careers or you've been out of the workforce for a while, consider jobs that will allow you to take several months off at a time. Or think about restructuring your present job so that taking time off will be easier.

Many occupations are ideally suited for taking long breaks, says Kathleen Tucker, host of the Travel Forum on America Online, a computer on-line service. "Teaching is an obvious choice, but there are plenty more," says Tucker, who once worked as a tax preparer and took time off during slack periods to travel. "Occupations like real estate sales, accounting, photography, and construction work generally pay well and often have built-in slow periods."

Many people, of course, have fashioned careers that allow them even more time off. "There's a new breed of temporary or interim managers and professionals who have expertise in a certain field and work only on assignment, giving them built-in free time," Tucker says. "At my husband's school, they've hired an interim headmaster while they search for a replacement for the former headmaster. He works a year, then travels for a year, then works again someplace else."

It's not just teachers who are doing it, either. Doctors, lawyers, businesspeople, clergy, and others are doing much the same thing. What's more, many of them are taking full advantage of the prevailing economic mood, charging a premium for their services. After all, employers are hesitant to hire full-time permanent workers in uncertain times, but they're often willing to pay more for someone with special skills who is working on a temporary basis.

Do Something That Has Future Value to Your Employer, Your Customers, or You

As you'll learn in Chapter 4, you often can negotiate for the time you'll need—or justify taking the time yourself if you're self-employed—by doing something that pays long-term dividends. Many college professors, for example, now routinely take up to several years off from teaching to get hands-on experience in business. An executive for IBM takes a few months off each year to take up his duties with the Utah legislature. Others have taken time off to explore first-hand new markets for their products or to update their skills.

Jim Bagley took two years off from his own advertising business to build a house near Albuquerque, New Mexico, saving himself many years' worth of inflated mortgage payments and making himself more marketable to boot. "How did I do that?" he says, laughing. "It's funny, but the business I'm in really is about solving problems. And in building that house I became very good at making quick decisions, making a lot of decisions, and learning to live with those decisions. I'm a lot more confident now."

HURDLE #3: BUT MY FAMILY AND COWORKERS WILL NEVER GO ALONG

Unless you're a loner, an orphan, or both, you'll need to win more than your boss's favor to ensure a successful sabbatical. You'll also want to involve your friends, family, and coworkers in your plans. That's especially true if you're thinking of taking any of those folks along with you or expect them to pick up some of the slack while you're away. How do you do it?

Make It Easy on Those You Leave Behind

No one, either at work or at home, wants to be left holding the bag while you're off sitting on a beach in Tahiti, sipping rum out of a coconut. Put simply, they'll resent it. And they'll make your life miserable when you get back.

The simplest way to avoid that kind of trouble, of course, is to lessen the load for those left behind. At work, for instance, you might arrange for an intern fresh out of college or graduate school to help out for a few months in exchange for a glowing future reference. Or you might hire a temp to come in—if only once every few weeks—to handle some of your regular duties. Similarly, you can often avoid hard feelings among friends or relatives simply by planning ahead and lavishing them with thanks. If you want your sister to send in your mortgage or rent payments while you're away, make out the checks ahead of time, along with addressed, stamped envelopes. If you want a friend or neighbor to take care of your cat while you're gone, make sure you leave behind plenty of kitty litter, cat food, *and* those tickets to the symphony.

Jan Griffin, an Episcopal priest in San Francisco, went out of her way to make sure her four-month sabbatical didn't leave her church in the lurch. Her solution? She asked a former nun she knew to pitch in during her absence in exchange for a small stipend—a decision that paid off for everyone involved. By going out of her way to find someone with plenty of experience doing counseling and handling other routine church duties, Griffin let the rector and the congregation know she was thinking about them and doing what she could to take care of *their* needs.

Be Willing to Compromise

You say Montana; your kids say Bahamas. Or you want to bicycle through Ireland, and he wants to climb mountains in Chile. What are you going to do?

Don't call the whole thing off, says Marcia Lasswell, a psychology professor at California State University and family therapist in Los Angeles. Instead, *compromise.* "There's frequently a way to satisfy both sides," she says. The couple who can't decide whether to go biking in Ireland or mountain climbing in Chile, for example, might split their sabbatical into two equal parts, she points out, spending half in Ireland and the other half in Chile. Or they might agree on a single location where they could both easily do what they want.

Lasswell recalls one couple she counseled who simply had different styles of traveling. He was rigidly organized; he wanted to travel a set distance each day without stopping, and he wanted to know ahead of time where they would be staying and what the arrangements would be for dinner. She liked to travel without a schedule, stopping wherever things looked interesting. "With my help," she says, "they agreed to take turns being in charge. On her day, they would travel her way. On his day, they traveled his way. And they had a great time!"

Sometimes all it takes is a little creative problem solving. After years of teaching high school mathematics in Waynesburg, Pennsylvania, Ellen Boros was ready to hit the open road. Everything seemed set: her school would pick up half her salary for the six months she planned to be away, and she had recently bought a used van fitted with many of the comforts of home, including a sleeper compartment and refrigerator. There was just one problem. Her boyfriend, a carpenter who was just getting a new career off the ground as a ceramic artist, wasn't at all sure he wanted to go. He didn't think he could spare the time. Instead of getting angry, Boros came up with a solution: Why not combine her sightseeing trip with his career goals? Specifically, she suggested that they rejuggle her itinerary to include stops at art galleries in major cities across the country. It worked; they both had such a good time that they started planning their next sabbatical as soon as they got back, and he received several offers to show his work as a result of the personal contacts he had made.

Get Others Involved

Start at the very beginning by giving those most affected by a sabbatical a role in either shaping it or participating in it. For example, you might give a subordinate at work a chance to take on a larger role in your absence, with the understanding that the new responsibilities will be permanent. Or you might appeal to an even more basic self-interest. Nancie Thomas, a junior attorney in Washington, D.C., helped convince the beleaguered partners in her law firm to give her six months off by volunteering to be a kind of human guinea pig. If this works for me, she told them, it can work for you.

Don't expect those closest to you to be excited about a sabbatical if they aren't willing participants. Family members, in particular, need to be involved early. "You'll pay if you don't," says Lasswell. "Especially if you have kids. A child who is dragged out of school and leaves friends behind for *your* idea of a good time can get pretty ugly about it," she says. Her solution: lots of advance work.

Lee Belfiglio, a viola player in the Seattle Philharmonic Orchestra and the mother of two young sons, spent more than a year planning her family's three-month cross-country car adventure, making sure she involved her family every step of the way. "The first thing we did was get this huge map of the United States, which we hung on one of our family room walls," she says. "And then we just started planning our route and filling a huge, monster notebook with ideas for our trip. It was really this great family project."

Lisa Price, an assistant manager for a big veterinary warehouse in Pennsylvania, convinced her recently widowed mother that taking three months off to hike the Appalachian Trail wasn't an insane thing to do by enlisting her help. She asked her mother to send food and other supplies to designated points along the trail. "When I first broke the news to her about my plans," says Price, "she just looked at me and said, 'If you'll go see a psychiatrist, I'll pay for it.' But after she got involved, she really got enthused; she started bragging to all her friends about what I was doing."

Even a small role can make a big difference. One of the reasons New York masseuse Deborah Harse's regular clients have remained so loyal to her through the years, she says, is that they love hearing her stories about her trips to exotic destinations. And she accommodates them with detailed yarns that make them feel part of each new adventure. "As soon as I get back, all I have to do is call them," she says. "They're always excited to hear from me."

HURDLE #4: I CAN'T DO THAT!

A lack of cash, time, or support may be the most obvious stumbling blocks between you and six months of bliss. But if you're like most people, it will be a less obvious hurdle that will stop you cold in your tracks: yourself.

"The unknown is terrifying for most of us," says Cornelius Bull, president of the Center for Interim Programs, a Boston firm that arranges internships and sabbaticals. "It's a very threatening double whammy because it also represents change. That's why most people think a sabbatical is out of reach. It's not the money that's the snag. It's not the kids that are stopping them. It's that tape that plays in their head that says, 'I can't do that.' "

The trick to overcoming those fears is to separate real obstacles from the ones most of us conjure up out of our own insecurities. If you keep saying to yourself, "I can't take a sabbatical because I have a mortgage" or "I can't do it because I have kids," you're starting backward. You have to start out by asking yourself what it is you really want to do and then ask yourself, "Now how do I find a way to do that?"

Outsmart Your Fears

Bob Waterman, a venture manager and the coauthor of the best-selling book *In Search of Excellence*, applied that lesson himself nineteen years ago when he decided to take a nine-month backpacking tour of Europe and northern Africa with his wife, Judy, and their two children, ages 11 and 13. At the time, Waterman was 39 years old and just about to finish up a three-year stint running the Australian office of McKinsey and Company, an international management firm. The trip, he thought, would be a terrific way to spend some time with his family before returning to the home office in San Francisco to take on a new assignment. As the date of his sabbatical approached, though, one of his bosses let him know that he was simply too valuable to do without for nine months and hinted that, if he went through with it, his job might be in jeopardy. Waterman talked it over with his wife, took a deep breath, and went anyway.

What convinced him, he says, was a combination of stubbornness and sheer logic. "I didn't know if I'd still have a job with McKinsey when I got back," he says. "But I was very sure about my own skills. I figured the only real security I had was my own ability."

As it turns out, Waterman's confidence turned out to be

well placed. His boss at McKinsey relented, and he went on to have a long and successful career there.

One of the best antidotes to the inevitable fears that accompany change is careful planning. Kevin Condit, a marketing director for a Philadelphia database direct marketing company, fretted for nearly six years about taking a four-and-a-half-month, cross-country bicycling trip before he finally took the plunge. "The biggest obstacle was myself," says the 36-year-old Condit. "Once I had myself under control, everything else fell into place."

What finally got Condit over the hump, he admits, was breaking down the entire sabbatical—an elephant of worries and details—into manageable bites. He went step by step through every excuse he had given himself for not going: what he would do with his car, where he would live when his sabbatical was over, how he would store his belongings, how he would pay for the trip. "I went for a long walk and just logically thought through what I wanted to do and how I would do it," he says. To his surprise, he found that he had a ready, practical answer for every problem he came up with. "Once I thought everything through, deciding to do it was easy."

Careful planning often pays an unexpected bonus. As you work out the details of how and where you'll spend your time, the specifics of the sabbatical begin to generate their own enthusiasm. Suddenly it's not just a vague span of time you're daydreaming about; it's concrete achievements and experiences you can almost taste and feel.

A born organizer, Lee Belfiglio spent an hour or so each day plotting out the details of her family's 7,000-mile cross-country odyssey, from arranging a game of bocci ball in St. Louis with her husband's relatives to planning a week of horseback riding with some friends who live near Yellowstone. "I am probably the most organized person you will come in contact with," she says. "Everybody just hates the daylights out of me."

Make Your Plans Public, and You'll Make Them Real

Even the simple act of telling people about your plans can be an effective strategy for mustering courage. Attorney Nancie Thomas wanted to take a six-month unpaid leave from her law firm to travel throughout Southeast Asia but was worried that she wouldn't have the gumption to go when the time came. "I knew my single biggest obstacle was me," she says. "What if I didn't fulfill my expectations? What if I came back and they didn't let me have my job back and I had to sponge off my friends?"

To overcome her doubts, she told everyone she knew about her plans. "I figured if I told enough people, I wouldn't be able to back out," she says. "I know that makes me sound like a spineless person, but it worked. Everyone was so excited for me, and that excitement just sort of overtook any apprehensions I had."

Dorothy Gantz, a 39-year-old social sciences teacher in Little Rock, Arkansas, found the courage from her own fears to join the Peace Corps. "What really made me go ahead with it was my fear that I might go through life without ever contributing anything that was really meaningful," she says. "I didn't want to wake up at age 65 and say, 'God, why did I never do that?' "

That's also what finally convinced Shelly Zipadelli, a 33-year-old computer systems analyst from Connecticut, to take a five-month leave of absence from the Aetna insurance company. She'd always wanted to be a singer and actor but was reluctant to leave the security of a good job and a close-knit family. She finally talked her employer into the leave when she realized that unless she went to New York City and put her ambition to the test, she would always wonder about what might have been.

"I agonized over the decision," Zipadelli says, three months into her leave. "I went back and forth over it. But now that I'm here, my only regret is that I didn't do it sooner. I love what I'm doing; it's what I call the happiness of pursuit."

As it turns out, Gantz and Zipadelli may even have science on their side. According to a series of studies conducted by researchers at Cornell University, the biggest regrets in life arise not from failures *but from those things left undone*. Actions that turn out badly may sometimes cause more pain in the short run, says Thomas Gillovich, one of the researchers, but it's our inactions that we regret in the long run.

Bob Waterman missed out on a possible promotion that came up during his absence but had no regrets then and has none now. In fact, he not only credits the sabbatical for cementing his relationship with his children but for much of his later success as well, both at McKinsey and, eventually, as an entrepreneur and writer. The time away gave him a keener, fresher perspective. "It was absolutely invaluable," he says. "It allowed me to get out of my old skin for a while and see things from the point of view of a customer."

How does Waterman rate the time he spent away from work compared to his later successes? "In terms of a life-changing experience, I'd put it just below my marriage and the birth of my children," he says. "And then somewhere much further down the list, I'd put the success of *In Search of Excellence*. The book and my success at McKinsey and starting my own business gave us the money to do some things, but that time away was just enormously satisfying. It was a great adventure—everything from skiing down mountains we never thought we could handle to being thrown in jail together in Egypt. In fact, nineteen years later, I can still recall what we did each day for those nine months. How often does that happen to people?"

2

How to Choose the Break You Need

If you were given six months off—all expenses paid—to do whatever you like, what would you choose?

Maybe you'd like to walk across England. Or perhaps jerry-rig an old Nissan Pathfinder and drive it from Paris to Dakar. Or rent a house in Ireland and play traditional music. Or head off to Zagreb to aid in the war-refugee effort. Or maybe just crawl into bed with the complete collection of Jane Austen. The problem, you quickly find, is not a lack of possibilities. It is, instead, a veritable ocean of choices.

The solution is an elegant and intriguing one: get to know yourself as you never have before.

Begin by approaching your time off the way you might approach any big decision: hatch a big idea, research the subject, get advice from knowledgeable people, ask what your friends and family think, determine what you can afford (in both dollars and days), and then make some inevitable, though not necessarily hard, compromises. Do all this carefully and the right time off will gradually float to the top.

So grab a pencil and several sheets of paper, and prepare yourself for some intensive—and intensely enjoyable—

brain-storming. Once the metaphorical skies are clear again, your sabbatical choice should be, too.

STEP 1: WHAT WILL YOU DO?

First, pick a quiet time, a Sunday afternoon or an early evening out on the balcony, to sit and think about what you might do with your time off. Bring along any adventure brochures you may have stuffed away, prospectuses on fellowships you've dreamed of applying for, notes you've written to yourself about big ideas or getaways, coffee-table books about your favorite places or pastimes, maybe even your high school and college yearbooks. Take a deep breath and lean back. You'll soon begin writing down anything and everything you can possibly imagine doing on an extended break. If you're planning a sabbatical with your family or a friend, you might try this as a group experience.

Don't censor any ideas or do any naysaying at this point. The aim is to generate volume, not to distill. If it helps, think of this step as driving a car at night with the headlights on. Since it's dark outside, you can't see your final destination at first. But the simple act of driving through the darkness illuminates areas you wouldn't have seen otherwise. Likewise, the simple act of writing down random thoughts will lead you to ideas you hadn't imagined.

Your list might contain some generic sabbatical goals, such as "Learn an exotic language," "Help the poor," "Win the such-and-such fellowship," or "Get into shape." But before you start scribbling more of your imaginings, read on for a bit. We've assembled a batch of idea-generating techniques that you may not have considered.

Create an Extensive Self-Profile

What likes, dislikes, and attitudes define you? For example, do you prefer the outdoors? Do you blossom at the notion of devoting yourself to the arts? Are you a stoic loner who thrives in wide-open spaces, or do you crave more time with your buddies? Is there a certain challenge that would test your skills to the maximum—but that you've not yet found the time to try?

Write down all the traits that describe you. Add to that list any special skills or talents you possess. Then combine your entries into some logical groupings and see what experiences or activities they translate into. Let's say your descriptive list features "like to be in charge," "a generous person," and "gutsy" and your skills list includes "good with tools" and "a whiz at math." Maybe the group Habitat for Humanity could use you for five or six months. (See Chapter 3 for details.)

Or take an expandable folder and, over a period of a month, write notes to yourself about anything that captures your imagination—a movie, a newspaper article, a TV documentary, a memorable experience, a long talk with someone—and put those notes in the folder. At the end of the month, empty the folder, spread the notes out over a big table, and group together the ones that are part of overall themes and patterns. What might have seemed to you a collection of random thoughts could turn out to have sublime order and symmetry.

Take the case of Sean Plottner, a magazine editor. More than a year before Plottner embarked on his five-month African odyssey, he assessed the pluses and minuses of his current situation, his finances, and his job, and asked himself the question, "How can I make myself happy?" "I wrote down things that I wanted to do, mostly deep-rooted things," he says. "I wanted to learn to fly. Climb a mountain. Do some serious whitewater rafting. A lot of my thoughts had to do with the outdoors—crazy adventures. I even put down something like 'more exercise.' I realized that a lot of these things could be done, and if you added them all up, they equaled a major trip."

Take a look at what other people have tried as a way to jog your own ideas. Sabbatical counselor Cornelius Bull sends a list of opportunities to new clients. "When I sit down with people," Bull says, "I don't think most of them have any idea what's out there. But if you give them a lot of options and ask them to talk about them, more often than not they'll see something that they hadn't even thought about that turns out to be exactly what they're going to do." By having clients go through a list of thirty-two varied options, Bull says he gets an idea of what sorts of experiences he should hunt up for them. And those same clients are able to recognize opportunities that may not have been clear before.

Revisit Your Childhood Dreams

Turn the clock back to when you were 10 or 12 years old. If someone had asked you to name your future occupation, what would you have said? Okay, take "astronaut" and "president" off the list. Do any of the other jobs still appeal to you? Can you update them for the nineties? If so, write them down. You might try tracking down people you knew as a kid. Not only parents and family members but friends from your yearbooks, store owners you used to visit, people who knew you well. By telling them of your future plans, you fulfill two purposes: first, those people, when found, are absolutely enchanted to hear from you; and second, they usually have fairly vivid memories of what you used to talk about as a child—things that you may have submerged later in life because there were other expectations. Maybe you spent your youth putting on plays in the backyard—and perhaps it's not too late to enroll in drama school. Or perhaps you thought you'd ford the world's greatest rivers when you grew up—and could now plan an expedition down the Nile.

Ask Yourself What You'd Do If You Had Only Six Months to Live

Few imagined scenarios will better focus your thinking about your real priorities in life than the one in which your life is about to end. On your deathbed, what are your regrets going to be? You're probably not going to regret the things you did but rather the things you *didn't* do. You're not going to say, "Gee, I wish I had advanced my career in 1996," or "Gee, I wish I had visited fewer foreign countries or learned fewer new skills."

You might divide the "things I must do before I no longer exist" list into several categories: (1) goals that you absolutely, positively must accomplish before the end—these are your likely sabbatical plans: (2) things you would have liked to have done before departing—these might be folded in; and (3) parts of your lifestyle you'd stop doing right away if you had only six months left—this may help solidify your decision to leave behind your regular life for a while. They don't have to be grandiose achievements, like sailing the Pacific solo or climbing to the highest point of elevation in each of the fifty states. Your goal could be simply to write the history of your hometown or drive a camper to all of California's state parks or spend the summer with your oldest daughter before she goes away to college.

So far, the strategies we've discussed have asked you to look inward. The next few will externalize the process a bit more.

Consider Making Your Pastime into Your Time Off

What are your hobbies? Maybe you can ratchet them up a few notches. If you're really good at something, you might find it gratifying to seek out tougher competition in a place where the surroundings are less familiar and the stakes are higher. For example, if you like tennis, hook up with a high-powered pro for a few months of lessons and start entering city tourneys. If you paint, take five months and do nothing but that, and then start offering your efforts at art and crafts shows. If you're not a smashing success, so what? You had fun trying and have honed a lifelong skill. And after all, nobody says you have to junk your present career and rely on your hobby to cover the mortgage—though wouldn't it be poetic if things turned out that way?

Take the case of Kite Giedraitis of Portland, Oregon. He was a computer programmer, but deep inside he saw himself as a full-time marimba player. Finally, he quit his computer job, went on a year-long sabbatical to southern Africa to hone his musical skills in the instrument's homeland, and embraced marimba playing as a life's occupation. "I passionately love it and I can't imagine life without it at this point," says Giedraitis. Today he teaches marimba back in Portland and is a founding member of the Village Spirit Marimba Band.

Look at Your Present Job—and Do the Opposite

If you're deskbound, consider heading for the Colorado River rapids. If you're a newshound who chases blaring sirens, maybe you'd like a few months of quiet contemplation in a Southwestern desert or at a French university. If you work with numbers all day, taking a creative-writing course at a local college or pumping prose into a PC might be your ideal escape. If you're wired to the information superhighway, give yourself a tactile, "acoustic" break, such as digging up ancient bones or planting trees. Why? Because leisure experts have found that our personal growth and happiness go up when we push ourselves to the level of discomfort. Take outdoor adventures, for example. People whose first inclination would be to step away from adventure experiences may find it's just what they need, says Dr. Al Wright, professor of leisure studies at California State University at Northridge. By stepping into a world where they don't traditionally view themselves as participating, they increase their levels of discomfort and anxiety. And this is good? Well, yes, says Wright. "There's real benefit for people's personal development to take some risk. Frequently it's at those moments when we may discover some of our most important and telling insights." Often, too, there's a renewed sense of empowerment. You might say, "Well, if I could climb this mountain or navigate that river I can go after a new job or make a big change in my life once I'm back."

Make History

Consider accomplishing some feat or record that gets your name inscribed in print, on a shiny metallic substance, or in the memories of those who share your area of interest. You'll find scads of prescribed trails, races, routes, marks, and challenges out there for the conquering. Consider concocting a landmark quest of your own—such as running or walking across your state or region along one of its blue highways, eating your way across the country via legendary barbecue shrines (and writing a book about it), or retracing the route of famous explorers or conquerors, such as Lewis and Clark's trek through the West.

Scott Erickson wasn't out to win a mention in the *Guinness Book* or a guest's slot with David Letterman when he hiked the perimeter of Lake Superior for nearly six months in 1985. Still, the feat positively altered the course of his life, if not history.

"I'd been reading books about long-distance hiking trips and in the meantime I really sort of fell in love with Lake Superior after some visits up there. In the back of my mind, I'd been thinking, Boy, it would be great to see the whole lake. And one day at work, the idea came to me for the first time, 'Oh! A Lake Superior loop ... and a hiking trip!' I knew right then, 'Yeah, I can do that and will do it.' Those two threads—a long-distance trip and Lake Superior—had been running along, and then they came together and it was like, 'That's it!' "

STEP 2: WHERE WILL YOU DO IT?

Where will you land? Do you want to stay close to home or go far away to a culture where you can pick up another language? How important is it for you have quick access to modern amenities and services? Are you looking for a place where you'll feel the most relaxed, most challenged, or the most needed?

Think back to vacations you've taken in the past. Where did you really unwind or feel energized? What combination of circumstances was involved—open spaces or teeming streets, mountains or the beach, ancient ruins or wilderness, lush and green or hot and dry, towering cities or rolling farmland? Make a list of all the geographical, topographical, and cultural attributes that just seem to click with you, and then grab a world atlas and look for places that offer as many of those attributes as possible. For instance, if you crave green landscapes, history, amenities, accessibility, and regional diversity, want to get out of the United States, and don't want to learn a foreign language beforehand, then one clear choice is Britain.

Jan and Kim ColemaNesset, for example, combined Kim's yen for long-distance cycling (she'd biked across Europe previously) and Jan's yearning to explore the Amazon and climb Peruvian peaks into their biking-hiking-canoeing trip in South America. David Ginsberg of New London, Connecticut, turned his love of long-distance biking and a desire to help a charitable cause into an around-the-world, 24,600-mile bike trip that raised money for Oxfam, an international relief organization. Before his journey, he was in the paper-supply business; now he leads cycling trips for a living as a tour guide with Bike Vermont. Atlanta's Brenda Green—who'd had a strong interest in international business since her law-school days—wanted the experience of living overseas. So she took a sabbatical from BellSouth to become a Peace Corps volunteer in western Russia, helping nurture business development in the city of Togliatti.

Ask yourself how crucial the particular site of your sabbatical is to its ultimate success. Maybe it's as important for you just to get away as it is to accomplish a specific goal or learn a new skill. On the other hand, if your ambitions are oriented toward developing your talents but aren't place-specific, it might be wise to stick to the home front. You'll save loads of money, and your energies won't be depleted by the rigors of adjusting to a new environment and a lot of unfamiliar faces.

Choose More Than One

If you're having a hard time deciding among a few powerful longings, then don't decide: package them together. Say that on your list you highlighted "Go on long walks," "Start learning a new language," and "Immerse myself in a regional cuisine." So maybe you could take a walking tour of southern France, bringing along a pocket-size *Berlitz*, a prodigious appetite, and plenty of thick socks. By stuffing several different activities and goals into your sabbatical suitcase, you'll not only spice up your experience but the odds of your sabbatical turning into a washout decrease dramatically.

Or divvy up your time off into two or three separate periods. That's how Colorado Springs, Colorado, attorney Bruce Buell arranged a multifaceted, sun-and-service, three-month sabbatical in 1982: he spent four weeks in the South Seas with his wife and two daughters, then donated more than a month to free consulting on estate planning with senior citizens, and then organized a trust-accounts program designed to provide funding for legal services to indigent clients.

Look at the Bottom Line

Walking across England might cost $1,500 or more in expenses. Walking across Portugal, though, can probably be done for $500 or less. That's why it's important to consider location as well as activity. Look at the exchange rate, the contacts you may have there (having close relatives living in Paris could make it a better deal for you than knowing no one in Krakow), and the travel expenses to get there. Great package deals are available for trips to South America, for example, while any journey to Moscow is likely to be pricey. Finally, consider a stay in your own backyard. It could be that your urge to weave custom-designed rugs could be done as well in your hometown as in Vienna. (For more tips on money matters, see Chapter 1.)

STEP 3: HOW LONG SHOULD IT BE?

One of the great secrets of a sabbatical is that taking more time off is easier than taking *less* time.

How can that be? It's because most of us are so busy that even if we're able to wangle three or four weeks off, we'd still have to make up that time. Our choices are to kill ourselves working before we go—and deal with work hangover the first week—or come back to a desk that looks like Pompeii after the eruption of Mt. Vesuvius. But here's the secret. If a time off goes beyond a certain point, say, six weeks, someone else has to take up the slack. Your clients or your workplace will have to find a temporary substitute for you. Your tasks won't await your return; they'll become someone else's responsibility. And once your office has made that adjustment, it doesn't really matter that much how long you're away. That's why the workplace runs just as smoothly, for example, when a woman is away on pregnancy leave for six months instead of three; the systems are in place. (And before you start feeling this is too selfish, consider that this makes life better for your colleagues, too. If your work is being done, their work becomes easier.)

Okay, so now you're faced with a time span somewhere between six weeks and eternity. Here the science of deciding gets a bit more murky. Barbara Rattenborg, for example, deliberately chose a two-year hitch in the Peace Corps for her sabbatical because she wanted to be gone for enough time to "truly understand the culture of where I was living." In contrast, Milton Stewart, an attorney in Portland, Oregon, found that he was wary of a sabbatical of more than three months. "I respect firms that have both six months and one-year sabbatical programs," says Stewart, "but I think if we had a one-year sabbatical program at our firm, we would lose a lot of lawyers." Stewart believes that he and his wife's three-month-long journey to Europe was just right for them. "We were beginning to wish for home toward the end. When we got on the plane in Frankfurt, we were ready to fly home."

Form Follows Function

Blame it on the Romans and their rigid calendar, but when most people think about sabbaticals they think in comfortable time boxes: three-, six-, or nine-month-long sojourns. Erase that thought. Instead, figure out what function your sabbatical is trying to perform. Are you striving for a reflective look at your life and career? Then ask yourself how long it will take you to unwind from your current state of mind. Are you doing mind-broadening research or some project? Then carefully plot out—week by week—exactly what you think you can accomplish and ask for time off that accurately reflects that time. Are you planning to travel? Pull out a map, estimate the number of weeks you want to spend in each area, and add up the total. The main point is that your activities should determine your time off, not the other way around. When Karen Davis, a part-owner of Davis-Kidd Booksellers in Tennessee, took time off to travel around

Europe by herself, she knew that a minimum of six months was what she needed. "It was an adjustment to get away," says Davis, who had worked years of seven-day weeks getting her bookstore chain off the ground. "It takes a while. Even though your body is away, it takes a while for your mind to do it. And it takes a while for you to throw off the need for structure that work brings. At first, a sabbatical feels almost too free, too cut loose."

Choosing Between a Structured and a Free-Form Sabbatical

Some sabbaticals will tell you how long you need. Generally, sabbaticals fall into two rough categories: those that are structured and have a somewhat firm starting and ending time, and those that are open-ended. Hiking the Pacific Crest Trail (which must take advantage of the warmer months and be completed before the snow falls) is a good example of a structured sabbatical. So is enrolling in a language school in Madrid or winning a national fellowship. Open-ended breaks, in contrast, are either completely fluid ("Should I jump on this train to Switzerland now or linger at this flower-draped café another few hours?") or tied to an event over which you have complete control. These are activities like researching the black sheep in your past for a family genealogy project or renting a cottage in Key West. Look to your personal style. When one Silicon Valley executive took his long-awaited break, he found that he needed to know when he was leaving and when he was coming back, simply because structure made him feel comfortable. You may also find it easier to ask the boss for a break if you have a firm itinerary. After all, if the class you're taking starts 10:30 A.M., April 18, it's hard for someone to say they'd like you to stick around until April 23 to finish up a few more tasks. Others may find that breaking away from a schedule is the whole goal of the time away.

Decide When to "Start the Clock"

If you can, add at least a couple of weeks of mental "healing time" to the front end of your sabbatical, especially if you've just undergone a big life change or career setback (such as getting divorced or "downsized"). Inevitably, when you plug some initial downtime into your sabbatical, the creative, productive electricity that may have seemed depleted resurges with a vengeance. After Ann Baker (a pseudonym) of Charlotte, North Carolina, was laid off from her fabric-testing lab job several years ago, her dream was to start making quilts. Her reality was that she first needed a rest. "The first couple of months after I was laid off I don't think I did anything. I was tired from the job I'd been working," she recalls. "I would sleep late and read a lot and not get anything done, and I felt guilty about that. Then after those two months I would get so involved in working on a quilt that I couldn't stop. Someone would come down eventually and say, 'Are you going to eat dinner or go to bed or anything?' And I'd say, 'What are you talking about?' I'd be thinking it was 6 or 7 P.M., and it was really nearly 1 A.M. I was so wrapped up in what I was doing, it didn't matter."

It's best to think of your sabbatical as a journey, not a destination, which is just how the self-help experts tell us we should approach life in general. Don't forsake the depth and intimacy of your experience for some superficial deadline, and don't try to accomplish too many things in too short a span. In other words, if you can't satisfactorily tour the entirety of Great Britain in the three months you've arranged, then draw the line at Scotland. And leave lots of room for spontaneity, serendipity, whim, and chance. Make sure you have enough freedom within the context of your sabbatical to change direction so if you want to explore deeper one particular area, you can find the time to do that.

Now that you have a better idea of what you want to do, distill that list into five or so final options. Then write each of them at the top of its own piece of paper and, underneath, fill in the fine points: where you'd like to go, if anywhere; who, if anyone, you hope will accompany you; how many weeks or months you think the experience might last; what purposes and goals you want to set; and what schedule you want to follow. Then take a deep breath and prepare for . . .

STEP 4: THE REALITY CHECK

Here's where the specter of limits appears on the scene. Actually, it's a welcome intruder. After all, without some real-world parameters on your sabbatical imaginings, you could be tossed around in a blue-sky brainstorm until the opportunity for the sabbatical has been lost. Now, take each of the five final options and subject it to the following litmus test:

How much does money matter? Take stock of your savings account, credit-card balances, and investment portfolio, as well as loans or gifts you may be able to get from those close to you. Establish a ballpark figure for how much you realistically have available to spend or can save within a reasonable time. Next, compose a list of expenses for each of your chosen experiences—airfare and/or ground transportation, equipment, food, lodgings, incidental and medical supplies, phone bills. Jot down a price estimate beside each entry. It's best to err on the side of excess, especially if you'll be in a volatile environment. If you're considering some sort of package tour, internship, or work-study project, most of your expenses will be set in advance. Opposite the expenses, in a separate column, list all your assets: any salary you may receive during this time, the amount of money you might get for renting your house, and any grants or scholarships coming your way.

Once you have a pretty good idea of the total cost of each sabbatical choice, match it up with what you can afford. If the cost exceeds your budget by 20 percent or more, maybe you should eliminate the option or, better yet, revise your spending plans downward. After all, the experience of a lifetime shouldn't be shackled by money worries. There's usually some creative way you can realize at least part of your dream, even if your bank balance isn't cooperating. For example, if you're set on doing a bike tour, you might opt for dollar-friendly Mexico or Peru rather than Sweden or France. Likewise, you can drop the costs and elevate the adventure quotient of your trip by hiking rather than renting a car or by tent-camping rather than snuggling into inns. The bottom line is: unless you're really well off financially, you'll probably have to make some trade-offs and sacrifices and accept at least some minor inconveniences, no matter what sabbatical option you choose.

How will family and friends be affected by your plans? For each sabbatical idea you're entertaining, let any and all persons going along for the ride—or staying home without you—know exactly what's in it for them. The worst thing you can do to someone you care about is to drag him or her on your six-month epiphany or leave that person in a lurch while you're gone. If there's no way you can involve that person in your pursuit—yet you wouldn't think of going alone—try to find or help arrange some project or learning experience that he or she can engage in while you're there, or else pick another pursuit. When Flip and Shara Rubin spent seven months traveling throughout Europe, they took different paths during part of their journey. Flip went to guitar camp for three weeks while Shara spent time at an Israeli kibbutz. Then they hooked back up for pursuits they had in common.

Once you have a clear idea of your choices, talk up your plans with those in the know, especially folks who have blazed the sabbatical trails you're considering. How do you find these people? Call up clubs and associations devoted to your area of interest and ask their presidents, executive VPs, or communications directors for referrals. If you're working through a particular foundation or university to arrange your sabbatical, you should have no trouble getting in touch with past participants. Call, write, or E-mail for advice and perspectives (or set up an appointment to chat with them if they live close to you). Do the same with people around you whose opinions you respect. Are there others at your company who have taken extended time off? Even if you're not replicating their journeys or activities, they can provide valuable insight about what to expect both during your break and when you return.

There are also consultants who plan sabbaticals, such as Cornelius Bull. You might seek out the guidance of a career counselor, especially if you're using the sabbatical time to decide on or explore a different career path or to enhance your qualifications and advance in your present job. A CPA can help you determine whether the projected cost of your sabbatical is endangering your nest egg or your children's college-education fund. If you'll be venturing far from home, a travel agent can help you get the best airfares and can assess many of your other transportation and lodging costs to make sure you're not overspending. And if your sabbatical has an educational component, talk with a faculty member who specializes in your field of interest at a local college or university. He or she can judge the depth and value of your plans, suggest books you can read in advance, and—who knows?—maybe even provide first-hand details from a similar sojourn he or she took in the past. After all, academia is where the modern notion of a sabbatical originated.

Finally, throw a dinner party for your closest friends and ask their opinions on what sabbatical you should choose. You'll benefit in three different ways: (1) everyone there will have a great time; (2) you'll get an array of solid and creative ideas for your time off from people who know and like you; and (3) your friends will feel a part of the decision-making process rather than ignored or abandoned when you embark on your sabbatical.

STEP 5: AND THE WINNER IS . . .

Okay, your brainstorm has moved well out over the Atlantic now. The numbers juggling and soul searching are over. You've got a few concrete options for how to spend your sabbatical. So pick one. If there doesn't seem to be a clear choice, sleep on the decision. There's no magic formula or mathematical equation for arriving at your ultimate choice. Just give your mind some space, and it'll whisper the answer in your ear.

Here's one last exercise you should try before you make any reservations or give notice to your boss or clients: test the water before you dive in. If you can afford and arrange it, take a one- or two-week scouting trip to preview your sabbatical: where you'll stay (or shouldn't stay), how much everything costs, how you'll get around, whom you'll be working or playing with, what extra stuff you may need to bring, even whether the vegetation makes you sneeze uncontrollably.

Let's say you plan to master a particular skill or area of expertise, such as computer programming or gourmet cooking. Maybe you can take a community college or university extension course on the topic before you commit to a more extended period of time. Harvard University, for example, runs a Career Discovery program where would-be architects and designers can spend six weeks deciding whether the field is right for them.

"If you give yourself a trial run, you'll feel a lot more comfortable," says Bull. He recalls putting that advice into practice himself when he was headmaster at a school in Arizona in the 1960s. Each year, as part of its curriculum, the school sent students to live for six weeks with Native American families on a reservation. An anthropologist suggested to Bull that the students spend three days with their respective host families well in advance of their eventual month-and-a-half stay. Those short visits made a big difference in diffusing the students' anxiety about the longer stays because, as Bull says, the longer stay became "a return to the familiar."

Now that your decision is in hand, don't hide it in a safe-deposit box. Start spreading the news. Tell everybody you know. Throw a party for yourself. Make a countdown calendar and stick it on your refrigerator, along with a few inspiring photos. Go to the library and check out every book that has anything to do with what you plan to do, and read at least a chapter every night before you fall asleep. Cook special theme meals for your family. But whatever you do, don't relax because, wherever you hope to go with your sabbatical, you've taken only the first few exuberant steps.

3

Menu of Fantasies

Before we go any further, permit us an analogy.

Say you were building a fantasy house—one that met all your needs, one that would be the envy of all your friends with taste. To come up with that house, you'd look at a lot of other houses first. You'd borrow the good ideas, reject some features once you saw them close up, and improve on other plans. You might rent a house for a few months that looked like your dream. Or you'd stomp through a lot of open houses over the weekends.

Deciding how to spend your sabbatical involves much the same process. Just by hearing about what others have done, you can start to shape your own getaway. And by taking a few steps down various hiatus paths, your own goals will start to crystallize.

We asked scores of sabbatical takers what they had tried and what they loved. Then we began compiling their ideas, along with dozens of others, to come up with the ultimate exhilarating time off for all interests. Here you'll find ideas for creative escapes, adventures, environmental pursuits, "inner work." Some of these programs will pay you to participate. Others offer life and career experiences that might propel you in a new direction. These ideas can get you started; it's up to you to take the leap.

THE CREATIVE LIFE

The Ucross Foundation

Imagine yourself as Billy Crystal in the film *City Slickers*. Instead of sitting in the saddle all day, you're at a computer or an easel. This residency program is for creative types who want to live temporarily in the American West while being struck by insights of brilliance. The retreat is located in a complex of buildings known as Big Red—built in 1882 and restored in 1980—in Wyoming's ranch country. Residencies are available to poets, prose writers, storytellers, photographers, printmakers, painters, filmmakers, video artists, sculptors, and composers. Participants are given private rooms in the renovated Ucross School House and individual work space.

Length: Two weeks to two months. Apply by March 1 for residencies between August and December; October 1 for residencies between January and May of the following year.

Fees: Free. Residents are responsible for their own transportation.

Requirements: Application form, résumé, project proposal.

Contact:
Elizabeth Guheen
Residency Program
2836 U.S. Highway 14–16 East
Clearmont, WY 82835
307-737-2291

Bellagio Center

If you're a scientist, policy maker, or scholar, this retreat nestled in the foothills of the Italian Alps gives you the chance to mingle with peers from around the world while working on "significant" projects. For the past forty years, the center has searched out people from countries around the world who have worthwhile scientific and scholarly projects. A companion program allows groups of two to five people from different geographic areas to work together at the center. It's a tough fellowship to win, but 140 people do so every year and you could be one—especially since the decision isn't based on who you are but, rather, what you propose to accomplish during your stay.

The center itself occupies a wooded promontory in northern Italy, on Lake Como. Surrounded by fifty acres of parks and gardens, the center's housing is in one of eight buildings dating back to the seventeenth century.

Length: Five weeks, any time from February to December. Apply twelve to fourteen months before preferred residency; decisions are announced seven to nine months before the period requested.

Fees: Free room and board. Residents pay their own travel and other expenses. Financial aid is available to cover those costs.

Requirements: Application form; half-page abstract summarizing the project to be worked on. Preference is given to those who expect their work at the center to result in publication, exhibition, or performance. Spouses (or spouse equivalents) may accompany residents at no cost.

Contact:
Susan Garfield
Bellagio Center Office
The Rockefeller Foundation
420 Fifth Avenue
New York, NY 10018-2702
212-869-8500

Cummington Community of the Arts

If you want to get away from it all, but not leave your family behind, this getaway in Massachusetts could be for you. Cummington is the only artists' colony in the States that is for both artists and their children. The campus is a lively one; twelve to twenty-four artists travel to the 150-acre site every month in search of living and studio space and, most important, a supportive environment. Evening meals are shared, and artists (meaning painters, video makers, dancers, and writers) gather afterward for readings and performances of their work. During July and August, children of the selected artists live together in a Children's Barn (better than it sounds) and participate in full-day art and nature programs.

Length: Anywhere from one to six months.

Fees: Each participant pays $700 per month. The fee for children is the same. Fees include a private studio and meals. Participants give five hours a week toward projects like gardening or preparing meals.

Requirements: Applicants must prepare work samples and a project proposal. If you're planning to bring along your child, he or she must be between the ages of 5 to 14.

Contact:
Cummington Community of the Arts
RR1, Box 145
Cummington, MA 01026
413-634-2172

Alden B. Dow Creativity Center

If you have an innovative idea that you think would work if you had time to develop it, this program could be a find. Located in the pastoral Saginaw Valley of central Michigan, the center offers four ten-week fellowships annually to creative people who can give a straightforward, detailed idea of their project. Some of the past winners created new math curricula, rethought residential health-care facilities, looked into the politics of the art world, and started creative-writing programs for prisoners. In other words, any creative idea with a devotion to quality and innovation can win.

Length: Ten weeks, from mid-June to mid-August.

Fees: Transportation to and from the center, a furnished apartment, and all meals are paid for by the center. In addition, each fellow is given $750 to spend at his or her discretion.

Requirements: Individuals in any field or profession who wish to pursue an innovative project or idea can apply. Upon completion of the fellowship, fellows give a verbal presentation of their project to the board of the center and then are sent on arranged media interviews to publicize their efforts.

Contact:
Northwood University
Alden B. Dow Creativity Center
3225 Cook Road
Midland, MI 48640-2398
517-837-4478

Master of Arts in Media Studies

The New School for Social Research, located in Greenwich Village in Manhattan, was founded in 1919 as America's first university for adults. That means that you won't see any fraternity houses or basketball teams. What you will see are men and women in their late twenties to early seventies who are temporarily stepping out of their careers to earn an advanced degree or switch fields. The school incorporates the Mannes College of Music and the Parsons School of Design. But one of the best hands-on programs is in media studies. Taught by working media professionals, the courses range from studying the documentary film to exploring the role of radio in American society. Your classmates will include people from all over the world, like Ciro Benedettini, a Roman Catholic priest and editor in chief of *L'Eco* (The Echo), a monthly magazine with a circulation of 130,000 published in Italy. He took a year off from his job in Rome "to make acquaintance with a new culture, the American media culture."

If you can't move to Manhattan for an entire year, you can still complete your degree. The New School On-Line Program allows students from all over the world to receive lectures, interact with faculty and students, ask and respond to questions, read assigned papers, and receive grades and comments, entirely through their personal computers and modems.

Length: One year (two semesters and an intensive six-week summer session) if you're seeking a degree. Nondegree candidates can take classes for as long as they wish.

Fees: Approximately $3,500 for full-time students. Housing costs separate. Some financial aid available. On-Line is $420 per credit.

Requirements: Although many students already have an undergraduate degree, that requirement may be waived for those with extensive practical experience.

Contact:

The New School for Social Research
66 W. 12th Street
New York, NY 10011
212-220-5600

London Theatre Program

If you're an Anglophile who loves the theater, this is nirvana. The program's goal is straightforward: to understand theater, you must see theater. In three and a half months, participants see an average of sixty plays and spend the rest of their days working and studying with top-rate British actors, directors, playwrights, and critics. On the days you're not sitting in the dark, you take numerous field trips throughout the country to learn more about British culture and the arts.

Length: Roughly September 13–December 4.

Fees: Approximately $4,600 per session. Includes housing and all meals. Airfare is on your own.

Requirements: If you want college credit, you must first enroll in Roger Williams University in Rhode Island (it coordinates the program). Otherwise, write directly to the program. Although most participants are college students, the program has also had members up to their sixties.

Contact:

London Theatre Program
Roger Williams University
One Old Ferry Road
Bristol, RI 02809-2921
401-253-1040

Paris Photographic Institute

Imagine photographing the great sights of Europe during the day and spending your nights in the cafés of Paris. This school, which draws its students from Europe, the Middle East, and North America, offers courses in every aspect of photography, from fine arts to commercial. You can be a professional trying to hone your craft or just an interested amateur. Part of your day is spent in a classroom or studio setting learning from professional photographers from around the world. The rest of the time is spent in the field, shooting fashion shows, conventions, and street scenes.

Length: The full-time program—sixty hours a week—lasts for two semesters. There's also a special five-week winter session.

Fees: Full-time is $6,500 per semester. The winter session is $2,000. Housing is extra and the school employs an agent who can help find apartments.

Requirements: From pros to beginners, all are welcome. Courses are taught in both English and French.

Contact:
Speos
Paris Photographic Institute
8, rue Jules Valles
75011 Paris
France
011-33-1-40-09-18-58 (phone)
011-33-1-40-09-84-97 (fax)

Salt Center for Documentary Field Studies

This nonprofit center has one goal: to document and record the lives and work of Maine's people. Since 1973, Salt students have roamed Maine, gathering material by interviewing lobster men in Tenant's Harbor, photographing third-generation blacksmith in Bangor, and talking with storytellers from Beal's Island. They've already accumulated more than 1,300 hours of tape-recorded interviews and some 100,000 photographic negatives. The center also publishes the striking black-and-white *Salt* magazine and four Salt books. It's located in a three-story brick townhouse built in 1849 in Portland, Maine.

Length: Twelve to twenty-four weeks.

Fees: $3,900 for summer semester; $4,900 for fall and winter. Room and board separate. Two-bedroom apartments cost approximately $400 to $500 per month.

Requirements: Most Salt interns vary in age, but many are either college students or recent graduates. If you're not interested in college credit, the center is open to nonstudents also. And if you're already a particularly gifted writer, photographer, or historian, you can apply to be a guest faculty member for a semester.

Contact:

Salt Documentary Field Studies
19 Pine Street
P.O. Box 4077
Portland, ME 04101
207-761-0660

New York Film Academy

What if eight weeks from now—without any experience in filmmaking—you could write, produce, direct, and edit your own ten-minute film? At this school, affiliated with Princeton University, students from all over the world work in small groups with terrific filmmakers to learn the art of cinema.

Students are assigned to groups of three or four, and they split their time between hands-on classroom instruction and location work. While you're in the field, you are helped by the Flying Squad, staff members who work on the set with students. Conditions are strenuous: participants work from nine to five, six days a week (or more). At the end of the two months, there's a final screening and party for friends and family, and you get a 16 mm copy of your work to take with you. Other courses include a fourteen-week evening workshop and another at Princeton during the summer months.

Fees: About $5,100 for the basic eight-week course (includes tuition, equipment usage, film, and processing) and the fourteen-week advanced course. Fee doesn't include housing or food.

Requirements: Obviously, any reading or work you can do on filmmaking beforehand helps. But instructors expect everyone to be a beginner. Classes begin and end throughout the year.

Contact:
New York Film Academy
100 E. 17th Street
New York, NY 10003
212-674-4300
212-477-1414 (fax)

Centrum Artists in Residence

If you're an architect, musician, writer, artist, or printmaker, you're eligible to apply to this nonprofit organization that maintains individual cottages on the Strait of Juan de Fuca in Washington. If you're selected, you stay for one month in a cozy, furnished cottage on the 445-acre grounds of Fort Worden State Park, a restored Victorian military base on

Puget Sound. And during that time, you can attend the festivals, performances, and conferences run by this arts and education organization. And what's expected of you? Just that you create great things.

Length: One month. Applications must be postmarked by April 1 for residencies occurring September through January; October 1 postmark for residencies occurring February through May (there are no summer residencies).

Fees: Completely free. And residents are given $75 a week for incidental expenses.

Requirements: Applicants must prepare a résumé, project proposal, and work samples.

Contact:
Centrum
P.O. Box 1158
Port Townsend, WA 98368
Attn: Residency Program
206-385-3102

Cottages at Hedgebrook

In 1985 Nancy Nordhoff, a nice woman with money, bought thirty acres of farmland and woods on Whidbey Island in Washington State, with the idea of opening a hideaway for creative women. At Hedgebrook each writer has her own cottage of timber-frame construction settled back in the woods. Upstairs is a sleeping loft lit by a stained-glass window, and downstairs are a work area, a sitting area, and a kitchen. Writers spend all day being creative and then have communal dinners at night with the other writers at the farmhouse overlooking Puget Sound. It helps to be a published writer, but any woman with a strong commitment to writing can be considered. As the literature says, "we realize that one of the greatest obstacles for women is the chance to break away from their daily responsibilities long enough to get started writing."

Length: One week to three months. Application is due by April 1 for stays between July and December, and October 1 for stays between January and June.

Fees: Completely free. And there are travel scholarships for writers whose financial circumstances preclude a stay.

Requirements: Well, you have to be a woman.

Contact:

Cottages at Hedgebrook
2197 E. Millman Road
Langley, WA 98260
206-321-4786

French Culinary Institute

Do you know how to use a knife and fork? Don't answer too quickly. At the French Culinary Institute, that's the lesson plan for the first day of school. From there, you and your sixteen classmates, ranging from stockbrokers to librarians, start cooking. Over the next 600 hours, you work your way through each of the stations of the classic French kitchen: *garde manger* (salads and appetizers), *poissonier* (fish), *saucier* (meat), and *patissier* (pastry). You learn all aspects of running a restaurant, from understanding food costs to planning meetings, and you work in the kitchen of L'Ecole, the classic French restaurant run by the school. At the end of the six-month program, you either start interviewing for chef jobs at swanky restaurants or return to your previous life—and quickly make it onto the "A" list of dinner party givers.

Length: The full-time program (Monday through Friday, 8:30 A.M. to 2:30 P.M.) takes six months to complete. Part-time (Monday, Wednesday, Friday from 5:30 to 10:30 P.M.) takes nine months. New classes start every six to nine weeks.

Fees: Lots of fees, and it looks even worse if you convert it into francs. Tuition is $16,850 and includes uniforms (nifty ones), knives, tools, supplies, and textbooks. Financial aid is available to anyone who qualifies.

Requirements: All you need is a high school degree and a passion for chopping, slicing, and dicing.

Contact:
The French Culinary Institute
462 Broadway
New York, NY 10013-2618
212-219-8890
212-219-9293 (fax)

THE NATURAL LIFE

National Audubon Society Expedition Institute

At Audubon's traveling environmental college, students crisscross North America on specially outfitted buses for a year. They camp out each night and are expected to "actively learn from wilderness, rural and urban experiences, environmental projects and diverse cultures." Basically, it's a learn-as-you-go college as you travel with approximately twenty students (in what Audubon calls "learning communities"). Semesters are broken into different regions of the country, from the Pacific Northwest to the Canadian/New England semester.

Length: Up to four semesters (two years). Students are split between those taking a semester off from regular college or work and those taking the full graduate degree program.

Fees: One semester, including tuition, food, and camping fees, costs $9,753. A full year is $16,705. Some students rent out their houses or apartments during the year they're gone, so costs are about the same as what you might spend if you stayed at home. And financial aid is available.

Requirements: If you're looking for college credit, you need an undergraduate degree and must enroll in Lesley College. Otherwise, anyone is eligible.

Contact:
National Audubon Society Expedition Institute
P.O. Box 365
Belfast, ME 04915
207-338-5859

International Crane Foundation

Quick weeding-out quiz: You're standing in muddy ankle-deep water, dressed as a tall wading bird, and you're feeding raw crustaceans to your "children." Do you feel (1) happy, (2) sad? If 1 is your answer, then apply for an internship at this world center for the study and preservation of cranes. Interns receive intense hands-on training in caring for endangered cranes and general instruction in the restoration of prairie, savanna, and wetland communities. In general, interns already have some aviculture (if you don't know what that is, skip to the next item) experience. But volunteers, who lead tours and learn about the species in general, are welcome, too.

Length: Three-month internships run throughout the year. Volunteers can start at any time.

Fees: Interns are paid $250 a month and given free housing. Volunteers are just that.

Requirements: Most interns are in college or are recent

graduates (though the foundation has had older applicants). But volunteers come from all over the world and can be of any age or background.

Contact:
International Crane Foundation
E-11376 Shady Lane Road
Baraboo, WI 53913-9778
608-356-9462

Foundation for Field Research

If you've always dreamed of being an archaeologist, a primatologist, or a marine biologist, then here's your chance. This foundation is a nonprofit organization founded in 1982 to coordinate research expeditions. Essentially, it helps financially strapped scientists (that's about all of them) by finding ordinary people who are interested in donating their time to projects in sea turtle conservation, prehistoric archaeology, and forest conservation. The projects take place all over the world, from Australia to French Polynesia to Costa Rica. About 500 volunteers a year become part of these scientific expeditions.

Length: Anywhere from two weeks to six months. Projects start and end continually through the year.

Fees: Volunteers pay a share-of-cost contribution that covers meals, lodging, and ground transportation and provides for the researcher's expenses as well. It runs about $350 a week (less for long-term projects). Most costs are tax-deductible.

Requirements: Adaptability and perseverance are the most important traits. Essentially you're a labor force and funding source in one.

Contact:
Foundation for Field Research
P.O. Box 2010
Alpine, CA 91903
619-450-3460
619-452-6708 (fax)

Volunteers in the Park (VIP)

There are more than 1,000 parks and wilderness areas in this country, ranging from the Grand Canyon to Joyce Kilmer National Forest. And because funding has been cut drastically in recent years, they all need volunteers to do jobs that were once careers. The opportunities, as they say, are limitless. If you like people, you can be a campground host and spend your days talking to campers from all over the world. If you dislike people, you can become a back-country ranger and spend weeks roaming the wilderness on your own. Potential professors (or current ones) can lecture on the wildlife of the desert. And computer experts can set up programs for keeping track of plant species.

Length: Anywhere from three months to two years.

Fees: Most volunteers receive $40 a week for expenses (double that for parks in Hawaii and Alaska) and are given a choice of tent space, trailers, or cabins.

Requirements: The Park Service tries to match applicants' skills to the job, but it's easy to make an argument for nearly any position.

Contact: The park system makes volunteering a little more difficult than it should be. That's because there's no coordination between parks, and the list of jobs runs into the thousands. You have three choices: contact the Student Conservation Corps (P.O. Box 550-C, Charlestown, NH 03603), which places adults in expense-paid volunteer positions; get a copy of "Helping Out in the Outdoors" (American Hiking Society, P.O. Box 20160, Washington, DC 20041, 703-255-9308), which lists more than 1,000 jobs open now; or write directly to the volunteer coordinator of the park you're interested in (this is especially valuable if you're trying to work with a big-name national park, because they don't always list their jobs in the other sources).

The Italian Cycling Center

For the dedicated cyclist, a trip to northern Italy is like a pilgrimage to the Holy Land. It's the center of the world's greatest bicycle makers. It's the training ground for many of the top professional racers. And it's home to the Italian Cycling Center, an American-Italian facility located forty miles northwest of Venice, at the foot of the Pre-Alps. Casual riders, fitness riders, and racers all congregate here for three weeks to four months to explore Italy by cycle. Riders are grouped by ability (the best can join the professional Italian team that practices there and join their runs) and spend their days biking to medieval cities, castles, museums, open-air markets, and vineyards. Nights are spent at a small hotel located in a cool alpine valley, where the chef prepares meals like grilled trout, steamed vegetables with virgin olive oil, and homemade Italian breads. Side trips include a visit to the Scapin bicycle factory where riders can buy a state-of-the-art racing bike and have it shipped home. Owner George Pohl also mentions that life-long friendships have started at his center. As he discreetly puts it, "Italy has been particularly hospitable to our female cyclists. Three women now make their home there with local cyclists they met while at the Italian Cycling Center." Good news or bad? You decide.

Length: The center operates from May 1 through September 30. Most cyclists stay from three weeks to four months. Reservations should be made by April 29. After that date, you must call Italy before you register to find out if there is space available.

Fees: $90 per day pays for a private room, three hearty meals (including mineral water and local wines), and coaching and ride-leading services. Bicycles are available for rent for $8 a day. But many of the more serious riders fly over their favorite bikes with them.

Contact:

George Pohl
Italian Cycling Center
2117 Green Street
Philadelphia, PA 19130-3110
215-232-6772

THE MULTICULTURAL LIFE

The Russian School of Norwich University

Do you want to dance Russian dances? Or sing Russian songs in the shower? Or dream Russian dreams? This outstanding school says its students have done all that and more. Entering its thirty-fourth year, the Vermont-based school offers beginning and advanced Russian with an emphasis in language, literature, and linguistics. Most of the students are in education, research, government, and business and either plan long stays in Russia or hope to do business there. The faculty is Russian born, and the school conducts an annual symposium series at which scholars lecture. One year, for example, Aleksandr Solzhenitsyn spoke. It also hosts a Slavic Festival and puts on plays throughout the year in the language.

Length: June 10–August 2.

Fees: $3,200. Includes all courses and housing. Financial aid is available.

Requirements: A college degree if you're seeking course credit. Otherwise, just a keen interest in the language.

Contact:

The Russian School
Norwich University
Northfield, VT 05663
802-485-2165

Instituto Allende

This language school not only is the oldest and largest Spanish teaching foundation in Latin America but also has the superb benefit of being in the colonial mountain town of San Miguel de Allende, Mexico. This sixteenth-century town is full of cobblestone streets, splendid churches, and wonderful cafés. It's also a haven for American and Spanish novelists and artists—many of whom have temporary homes here during the year. Students at the institute take four- to six-month Spanish immersion classes and spend the other half of their time painting, weaving, touring, and learning about Mexican life and culture.

Fees: $1,200 to $3,600 for four- to eleven-week sessions. Includes room and board.

Requirements: If you're seeking college credit, you must currently be enrolled in a university. Otherwise, anyone may apply.

Contact:
Instituto Allende
San Miguel de Allende, Guanajuato
C.P. 37700 Mexico
(011-52) 415-2-01-90

Cemanahuac Educational Community

Another institute combining Latin American studies and intensive five-day-a-week Spanish lessons, this Mexican school also specializes in family immersion classes. Younger children attend bilingual school programs in Cuernavaca, the town where the institute is located. Children at the junior-high level and above study at the institute with their parents. Weekends are spent on field trips around the country. To get into the right mood, rent John Huston's classic film *Under the Volcano* for a look at the scenery. And once you're there, check out the recently active volcano—the town is nestled right near the often-angry Popocatépetl.

Length: Ten to sixteen weeks is the norm, though special one-week classes are available.

Fees: The ten-week quarter costs $1,460, plus tax. Housing with a Mexican family, including meals, is $14 per day. Children's fees are determined separately according to age.

Requirements: Special emphasis is placed on beginners, but advanced classes are available, too.

Contact:
Cemanahuac Educational Community
Apartado 5-21
Cuernavaca, Morelos
Mexico
(011-52-73) 18-6407

Scandinavian Seminar

This forty-year-old program offers a chance to learn a Nordic language while attending seminars on compelling international issues. The Semester Programs on Nordic and Global Issues offers small classes (made up of Americans, Brits, Australians, and Scandinavians) that focus on peace issues and sustainable development. The six months are spent at pastoral campuses in Scandinavia and at on-site meetings at castles, farms, and manor houses throughout the region. The beauty of this program is that you aren't placed in segregated classes ("Okay, all Americans over here"), but instead are allowed to immerse yourself in the typical daily life in that part of the world. As part of that goal, you live and study at a *folkehojskole*. Hard to translate, it's essentially a network of residential, adult educational institutions that offer one year of study that seeks to enlighten and educate rather than leads to a degree. In other words, you're learning for life, not for an exam.

Length: Six months, beginning in late July or early January.

Fees: $7,200 covers tuition, travel within Scandinavia, room and board, books, and an intensive language course that begins the semester. Some financial aid is available.

Requirements: If you're enrolled in a college at the time, just write away for information and then plan on sending your transcripts and recommendations. Nonstudents send letters of recommendations from current employers.

Contact:
Scandinavian Seminar
24 Dickinson Street
Amherst, MA 01002
800-828-3343

LEX America

There is a place where the Mighty Morphin Power Rangers have not taken over the countryside. Join this program in Japan, and you and your family can live with a Japanese family for six weeks. Your children attend typical schools with their Japanese "brothers" and "sisters." Your Japanese hosts make "my home your home" and teach you everything from how Japanese light switches and faucets work to the intricacies of the Japanese tea ceremony. And every week, you can meet with American families and individuals who are staying with other host families and compare notes. Participants have ranged from families considering a move to the Far East to individuals who want a closer look at this country.

Length: Anywhere from one month to six weeks.

Fees: $3,000 covers round-trip airfare from a West Coast gateway city, travel insurance, and all costs abroad.

Requirements: Because you'll be living in a home with a family, you'll need to be flexible in your day-to-day routine. Foreign-language skills are not required.

Contact:
LEX America
68 Leonard Street
Belmont, MA 02178
617-489-5800
617-489-5898 (fax)

La Sabranenque

If you took French in high school or college and always wanted to perfect it, this is your school. Situated in the southern French village of Saint-Victor-la-Coste, the school offers three-month immersion classes for speakers at the "low intermediate" level. On tap are the standard language school advantages: small classes, housing in historic buildings, a chance to speak with local inhabitants about their work and life (this includes wine growers, cheese makers, wild-bull herders, and so forth). But what sets this school apart is its restoration work. Students spend two half-days a week building and restoring a twelfth-century section of the village. Emphasis is on traditional manual building techniques. (In fact, you'll be housed in a structure that was restored by students in 1987.)

Length: Three months (roughly February 19 to May 13). Classes are held Monday through Friday, a total of thirteen hours per week.

Fees: The language-restoration project costs $4,500. Includes housing and meals. The restoration-only portion (approximately three weeks) costs $930.

Requirements: A working knowledge of French. Non-French speakers can sign up for the restoration project only. Participants work side by side with French and Italian restorers and learn stone masonry, floor and roof tiling, path paving, and stone cutting for window and door openings.

Contact:

Jacqueline B. Simon
217 High Park Boulevard
Buffalo, NY 14226
716-836-8698

International Hebrew Study Center
(Ulpan Akiva Netanya)

For the last forty-four years, this school has had a simple purpose: to encourage students, adults, and families to study the Hebrew language in its natural setting, Israel. You don't need to be Jewish (even agnostics are welcome, says the school) and age is irrelevant. But you do need a strong desire to learn more about this language. Participants attend programs of social and cultural activities three nights a week and often take field trips on weekends.

Length: From twenty-four days to twenty weeks. Sessions are staggered, with courses beginning year-round.

Fees: The twenty-four-day session runs about $3,500 if you'd like a private room; $2,500 if you're willing to share. The twenty-week session is about $12,000 for a private room; $8,300 if you have a roommate. Fees include all classes, full board (including three meals a day and a room on the beach), and a "study folder." Textbooks and in-country traveling costs are extra.

Requirements: Classes are open to anyone.

Contact:

Ulpan Akiva, Netanya
International Hebrew Study Centre
P.O. Box 6086
42160 Netanya
Israel

THE GIVING LIFE

Habitat for Humanity

This house-building organization has a simple goal: to have the affluent of the world build homes for the needy. By using volunteers and donations of money and materials, Habitat builds and rehabilitates homes with the help of the future homeowners. Then the houses are sold to the families for no profit with no-interest mortgages. The organization—which champions former president Jimmy Carter as its most famous member—is looking for construction workers (anyone with handyman skills), bookkeepers, public relation experts, and electricians. Positions are available in both the United States and abroad.

Length: Anywhere from one week to one year.

Fees: Habitat supplies room and board and a small living stipend to all its volunteers.

Requirements: Anyone who's willing to help.

Contact:

Habitat for Humanity
Habitat and Church Streets
Americus, GA 31709
912-924-6935

Institute for International Cooperation and Development

This global traveling school is modeled on the Scandinavian folk-education idea: to promote learning for the sole purpose of gaining knowledge and experience, not for fame or credit. Essentially, participants learn about the world by traveling to other countries and working with the local populations. For example, in Zimbabwe, the institute runs the Street Children School, which gives orphaned children (who've lost their parents in the civil war there) a place to live and learn during the day. In Mozambique, teams of workers have been creating eucalyptus plantations throughout the country (this tree grows quickly and is a good house building substitute instead of destroying hardwood forests). And in Brazil, they're building a rural cooperative for poor farmers in the north-eastern section of the country where farmers will be taught agricultural skills.

Length: Approximately one year, although a few programs are shorter. The first two to three months are spent at the institute's campus in the Berkshires, learning languages and skills. Participants then go overseas.

Fees: Approximately $3,200 for the year. This covers room and board, airfare, and training. You may also be asked to help the institute with fund-raising.

Requirements: The institute enrolls everyone from high school students to retirees to people thinking about changing their careers. They ask that participants feel an "obligation to help people in need" and have no fear of hard work.

Contact:
IICD
P. O. Box 103-F
Williamstown, MA 01267
413-458-9466

The Coro Fellows Program in Public Affairs

People with short attention spans, pay attention: here's a program that will let you try out five jobs in one year. The Coro program is a vigorous blend of internships, seminars, retreats, group projects, and interviews. The core of the program is a series of full-time internships with five organizations, each representing a different aspect of the public sector. You work with a government agency, a political campaign (timed to coincide with Election Day); a community agency; a corporation (so you see how the private sector is linked to the public); and finally, a labor organization. As a Coro fellow, you are trained to cope with the diverse problems affecting public-policy institutions. And you join a very prestigious alumni group, including Dianne Feinstein (the senator from California), Elizabeth Batov (the former treasurer of the United States) and Gene Siskel (movie critic).

Length: Nine months, from September to June. Along with the five internships, fellows meet twice a week (usually all day Friday and one weekday evening) for a seminar period.

Fees: $3,500 covers the cost. Coro does award living stipends of up to $10,000, however, according to need.

Requirements: Although some recent college graduates are among the fellows, many are people in their thirties and forties who are improving their careers or making a jump to a new one. The program is offered in four cities: San Francisco (the oldest, having started in 1947), New York, Los Angeles, and St. Louis. Submit your application to the center nearest your home, but you may be placed in any of the cities. About 400 people apply annually for the forty-eight spots.

Contact:
Coro Fellows Program
95 Madison Avenue
New York, NY 10016
212-248-2935

Vietnam Rainforest Inventory Program

This probably has escaped your notice, but in the past twenty-five years, Vietnam's forest cover has been depleted from an estimated 50 percent to 19 percent. The usual culprits are the reason: land clearance, logging, firewood collection. Add to this the nearly 2.2 million hectares of rain forest damaged or destroyed during the Vietnam War. Unfortunately, the Vietnamese government has neither the funds nor the interest to stop the destruction. That's where the London-based organization Frontier stepped in. This "conservation through exploration" group takes volunteers from around the world who are willing to work with local communities to stop environmental destruction. In Vietnam, for example, volunteers are mapping, acre by acre, the extent and condition of forest cover. This is a challenging program. You live in tented camps, eat locally grown rice and vegetables, and spend your days in remote and usually inaccessible regions. In exchange, you know that your efforts are contributing in a practical way to the future of the global environment.

Length: Three months. Projects start and end on a staggered schedule throughout the year.

Fees: Frontier asks for a "contribution" of between $2,500 and $3,200. This includes your airfare, medical insurance, accommodations, and food. They recommend the fees be raised through fund-raising, and they've compiled a booklet that explains how you should go about it.

Requirements: Volunteers come from all walks of life and all age groups. Many of the participants either work in or are considering switching to a career in conservation.

Contact:
Frontier
77 Leonard Street
London EC2A 4QS
United Kingdom
011-071-613-2422
011-071-613-2992 (fax)

THE SPIRITUAL LIFE

The Naropa Institute

This institute is the only accredited college in North America whose educational philosophy is rooted in Buddhist contemplative tradition. What that means is that right after you leave, say, your Business Administration of a Child Care Center course, you head on over to your T'ai Chi Ch'uan course. Situated on 3.7 acres in the center of Boulder, the college has approximately 650 students (most of whom are much older than the average college student) attending year-round. Of special note are the Study Abroad programs to Nepal and Bali, where students are immersed into the philosophy, music, painting, and dance of the regions.

Length: Nine months.

Fees: A year's full course runs about $8,000. Housing is extra. You can also enroll as a noncredit student for approximately half-price. The Study Abroad program costs $3,800 and includes lodging but excludes airfare.

Requirements: Open to anyone who's interested in the ways of Buddha and is willing to write a five-page typewritten, double-spaced "letter of interest." The twelve-week Study Abroad courses are open to any student or nonstudent. Applications are taken on a rolling basis during the year. Deadline for the Nepal trip is April 20 and the Bali trip November 1.

Contact:

The Naropa Institute
2130 Arapahoe Avenue
Boulder, CO 80302
303-444-0202

Insight Meditation Society

Shut off the TV. Turn down the radio. Close the windows. Stop talking. How does it feel? Now, try it for three months. At the Insight Meditation Society in tiny Barre, Massachusetts, an increasing number of professionals, corporate types, and others pay $29 a day to keep their mouths shut. Fall is the prime season, when the center begins its three-month silence. "It will change your life," says Phillip Moffitt, a former owner of *Esquire* magazine, who recently spent six weeks at the center. No doubt. Participants live as temporary Buddhist yogis, rising before dawn and starting meditation at 5:30. The rest of day, as described by *Wall Street Journal* reporter Ron Suskind, "sitting, walking, lunch, walking, sitting, walking, sitting, walking, dinner, sitting, walking, sitting, walking, sitting, late tea, with a last sitting ending at 11. There is no reading." Advocates speak of massive changes in their lives.

Length: Short sessions—from three to ten days—are possible, but the eighty-seven-day "long silence" is the most popular. The fall session is usually fully booked by the early spring.

Fees: $29 a day covers spartan accommodations and all meals.

Requirements: Strong, silent types are encouraged to apply.

Contact:
Joseph Goldstein
Insight Meditation Society
1230 Pleasant Street
Barre, MA 01005
508-355-4378

Desert House of Prayer

Even the name of this spiritual retreat appeals to those seeking a true getaway. Desert House seeks out those who wish to avoid being sought out. The complex is located on a stark, isolated thirty-one acres of primitive, high desert land, blanketed with desert plants, flowers, and trees at the foot of Safford Peak in the Tucson mountains. It has three mountain ranges in its backyard but only one telephone inside (as the owners say, "we presume that while on retreat you will want to drastically reduce the time you normally spend with this invention of mixed blessing"). Founded by a priest and two nuns some twenty years ago, the center reaches out to "the tired, those suffering from burnout or overwork, or who are dead emotionally." It offers prayer, communal meals, spacious private rooms, and a well-stocked library. And a promise that they will help you pursue "interior transformation."

Length: The most common retreats are two weeks to one year.

Fees: $27 per day for three months or less (this includes three meals a day). Longer stays are negotiated at a lower rate.

Requirements: Christians and non-Christians alike are welcomed. The center believes that certain individuals are "sent" to them for help.

Contact:
Desert House of Prayer
P.O. Box 574
Cortaro, AZ 85652
520-744-3825

Diet and Fitness Center

Duke University Medical Center runs one of the country's foremost serious weight-loss programs. You move to North Carolina for four weeks (many clients stay longer) and lose weight. Lots of weight. And if you're like the majority of their clients, you don't gain it back. That's because the center emphasizes a whole new way of life rather than a diet. Sounds like a brochure, but this place is for people who are sick of their weight and are willing to pay a large amount of money to lose it. Beyond the normal routine of lectures, moderate exercise, and motivation talks, participants are taken to the grocery store to learn how to pick out the right food, and they go on restaurant "field trips" to learn how to order. Patricia Farrell, a staff writer for the *Washington Post*, wrote, "Three weeks ago I could not walk two blocks for a sandwich. Today I walked three miles for a newspaper."

Fees: The four-week program is $4,795. That includes a complete medical examination, all daily classes, and three sensible meals a day. It doesn't include housing, which runs about $45 a night. Additional weeks are $525 per week and, later, drop to $425 per week.

Requirements: People who consider themselves twenty pounds or more overweight are welcome to attend.

Contact:
Duke University Medical Center Diet & Fitness Center
804 West Trinity Avenue
Durham, NC 27701
800-362-8446

Ferry Beach Unitarian Camp

Still smarting over your crummy camp experiences while growing up? Here's a chance to have a fantasy summer getaway—and take your kids along with you. The Ferry Beach Unitarian Camp is a thirty-five-acre campus situated next to sea and sand in the lush Maine woods. Every summer they offer an amazing array of programs for both children and adults, from Reiki classes to father-kid retreats to West African dance weekends. Combined with the classes is an emphasis on spiritual and intellectual growth and the (very voluntary) chance to attend daily religious services. Many of the participants have been bringing their families to the campus for years.

Length: While you can stay at Ferry Beach for as little as a weekend, the best bet is to stay the entire season, from June 23 to September 4. You can enroll in a series of classes and seminars or simply take some weeks off to walk the beaches or write long letters.

Fees: The most affordable route is to park your camper in the Hersey Grove—the peaceful campground across the street from the facility. An entire season costs $1,250. Add the classes, which range from $50 to $150 a week (kids' programs are $10 per day) and an annual family membership fee of $68. As an alternative, the Quillen Hotel, a mid-1800s inn, offers rooms for $18 a day. Three meals a day run another $22.

Requirements: All are welcome, regardless of religious background.

Contact:
Ferry Beach
5 Morris Avenue
Saco, ME 04072
207-282-4489

Abba House of Prayer

This 1920s-style house in an urban residential neighborhood in upstate New York began offering "spiritual sabbaticals" with great success starting a few years ago—over 150 people have come to the retreat for stays of one to eleven months. The two Roman Catholic sisters who run the facility say that it offers "the perfect opportunity for rest and renewal of body, mind, and spirit for persons who have worked hard, and need a temporary break from their regular heavy commitments." Plus, it offers these benefits: you can get up whenever you like in the morning (none of that pre-5 A.M. "aren't we all happy we're monks" business), you can read at the table during breakfast and lunch (which many people do, since talking is discouraged at these meals), and you can leave the facility during the day if you like and tour around the area via bus.

Length: Up to one year.

Fees: A private room and three meals daily is $600 a month.

Requirements: People of all religions are welcome. You must fill out an application that asks why you're interested in taking a sabbatical at this time and how you expect to use the opportunity.

Contact:
Abba House of Prayer
647 Western Avenue
Albany, NY 12203
518-438-8320

Holden Village

Want to explore your spiritual direction and polish your alpine skiing skills? Holden Village is a small former copper mining town—accessible only by boat—that was donated to the Lutheran Church in 1960. Since then, it's become a year-round Christian retreat nestled in the Cascade Mountains of Washington. Days are spent in daily Bible studies and conversations led by a variety of teachers who seek to place current affairs and concerns in the context of the Gospel. Free time is spent wandering around the small village (complete with libraries, bookstore, craft area, and bowling alley) and hiking and skiing around the area (the center says it has an annual snowfall of 220 inches).

Length: The ten-week Winter Sojourn is from October to December. A shorter session is available in February. Summer sessions begin in early June and are of varying lengths.

Fees: The ten-week Sojourns are $775. This includes housing in simple but comfortable lodges and three meals a day. A one-week stay is $226; a special sabbatical rate is $151 per week with a minimum of four weeks.

Requirements: All faiths are welcome. During the summer months, children from newborns to ten-year-olds can join the Narnia program for special Bible camp activities.

Contact:
Registrar
Holden Village
Chelan, WA 98816
(There are no phones at the village)

THE ADVENTUROUS LIFE

Overland Journey

You've seen all your neighbors driving to the local convenience store in their overland 4-wheel drives. How about a trip that actually uses what these vehicles were built for?

"Overlanding" typically involves fifteen or twenty people rambling across a continent in a specially modified truck. These trips, which can last well over six months, offer a no-frills, ground-level experience of huge chunks of Africa, Asia, Australia, or South America. Rather than the Ford Explorers we're used to, overland companies use retrofitted English Army Bedfords and German Mercedeses, toting a portable gas station (that's because there can be spots in Africa, for example, where you may have to go 2,000 miles between fuel stops). On the trans-Africa journey, the route typically begins in the casbahs of Morocco, heads south across the Sahara, goes through tribal villages in West Africa, travels the rain forests of Central Asia, safaris in East Africa, and winds up in Cape Town or Johannesburg. Now, this is no stroll in the park; this is for the big boys. This is tough. This is something that'll give you bragging rights in the most testosterone-laden of crowds. Up for it?

Length: Anywhere from four to twenty-six weeks.

Fees: From $3,930 to $5,710, depending on length.

Requirements: Be prepared to cook your own food, sleep out under the stars, negotiate with mountain chieftains, and, basically, walk the walk and talk the talk.

Contact: Two companies offer overland adventures—Encounter Overland and Guerba. Both are represented in the United States by the Adventure Center (1-800-227-8747). In general, you're given the choice of going from Nairobi to London or vice versa. Veterans suggest the latter—the truck tends to be better stocked.

Backdoor BB&B Tours (Bus, Bed, & Breakfast)

Here's an organized expedition through Europe that's drawn strong praise from past sabbatical takers. For twenty-two days, you travel on a specially equipped comfortable bus—with plenty of empty seats—through the major cities and countries of Europe. You travel in a full-size thirty-four- or forty-eight–seat bus (with a maximum of twenty-four travelers). As Back Door says, "with plenty of empty seats for you to spread out and read, snooze, get away from your spouse, or whatever." This is not a typical tour. As Back Door puts it, "travelers can enjoy the benefits of a fully guided tour without the regimentation and expense of it—and without the independent-travel hassles of driving, using trains, and finding hotels." In other words, you travel and get settled at each destination as efficiently as if you were on a tour, and then you break away from the pack and make your own discoveries. Participants in the past have used the trip as a low-cost warmup for a longer stay in Europe.

Length: In twenty-two days, you travel to Holland, the Rhineland, Munich, Bavarian castles, Venice, Rome, the hill towns of Umbria, Florence, the Italian Riviera, the Swiss Alps, French Burgundy countryside, and Paris.

Fees: The $1,800 cost covers all bus transportation, beds in double rooms in "simple, creaky, memorable, centrally located Back Door–style hotels," all breakfasts and six dinners, three travel books, and all tips.

Requirements: Participants range in age from 16 to 75, with most in their twenties to forties.

Contact:
Europe Through the Back Door Inc.
120 Fourth Avenue North
P. O. Box 2009
Edmonds, WA 98020
207-771-8303

Humla to Kailas

Take a good look at the words above. Bet you $5 that you don't know where either is located. But after a thirty-two-day trek through this ancient territory at the edge of Nepal, you'll have a first-hand appreciation of where you've been. Wilderness Travel, the group that leads this expedition, is known for its walking excursions throughout the world. This is one of their most ambitious cultural odysseys. You climb past homes adorned by Tibetan Buddhist prayer flags, trek the ancient pilgrimage route around Mt. Kailas, visit cliffside monasteries, and visit Potala Palace. If there's a place left on earth without a McDonald's, this is it. Not only will you visit one of the least traveled regions left but you're guaranteed to be thinner and fitter than when you began.

Fees: These trips are pricey; $5,200 covers all accommodations (either inns or upscale camping), varied fresh meals, tour guides, and most incidentals. It doesn't include international airfare.

Requirements: In general, you've got to be in good shape to accomplish one of these trips. But past participants say the scale of fitness ranges from avid walkers to triathletes.

Contact:

For an overall catalog (including ninety other trips on six continents):

Wilderness Travel
801 Allston Way
Berkeley, CA 94710
800-368-2794
510-548-0347 (fax)

Wandering Wheels

If you want to *experience* the American landscape rather than merely see it from behind a pane of glass, leave the hermetic isolation of your automobile and hop on a bicycle. Tooling down the road at a speed of about 10 miles an hour, you travel fast enough to take in the entire coast-to-coast panorama of the nation in about seven weeks, but slow enough to pull over and chat with the locals as you crank through their towns. One of the best long-distance bicycle touring companies around is Wandering Wheels, which leads transcontinental cycling trips from Seattle to Rehoboth Beach, Delaware (not to mention other lengthy jaunts from Florida to Canada and from California to Georgia). The route is designed to take you past some of the most dazzling scenery in America: the Cascades of Washington State, Little Bighorn, Mt. Rushmore, the lush, rolling farmlands of the Midwest, and the crinkled Appalachians of West Virginia. The highlight of the trek is the Norman Rockwell-like police escort that the group receives at the end as they pedal en masse toward the Atlantic. The organization is run by a non-denominational Christian group, but the religious connection is kept extremely low-key, and people of all persuasions are welcome. If there's an overriding spiritual belief among organizers and pedalers alike, it's in the transforming power of adventure.

Length: Seven weeks.

Fees: $2,095 for the Seattle to Delaware trip. It includes two hearty high-carb meals a day, lodging (you sleep in churches), and team T-shirts. The tour company also brings along a portable shower, portable kitchen, bicycle-repair-shop-on-wheels, and a van for those who need an occasional break from pedaling.

Requirements: You have to be fit enough to ride a bicycle 70 to 100 miles a day, day in and day out.

Contact:

Wandering Wheels

P. O. Box 207

Upland, IN 46989

317-998-7490

Pacific Crest Trail

Strap on your serious walking shoes. It's possible to walk from Mexico to Canada past some of the most striking scenery to be found in the world. The Pacific Crest Trail is an exquisitely demanding 2,638-mile scenic trail for hikers and horseback riders. Temperatures range from a torrid 90 degrees to below freezing—and that can happen in a single day of hiking. The trail passes through twenty-four national forests, six national parks, five state parks, and many acres of private land. This high-mountain trail averages a 6,000-foot altitude in California, 5,000 feet in Oregon, and 4,000 in Washington.

Length: For a continuous hike, assuming you cover fifteen miles a day, it will take you 176 days. You can also try the trek in one-month slots: Washington, 31 days; Oregon, 30 days; northern California, 30 days; central California, 44 days; and southern California, 33 days.

Fees: You'll need superb equipment for snow and desert conditions—a cook stove, great hiking boots with ankle support, a lightweight, weather-resistant tent, a good sleeping bag. Most hikers find they spend about $2,800 over six months.

Contact:
Pacific Crest Trail Association
5325 Elkhorn Boulevard
Suite 256
Sacramento, CA 95842
800-817-2243

Wrangell Mountains Wildlands

Here's an adventure that's perfect for both the environmentally concerned or escaped felons seeking a refuge. Your base camp is the town of McCarthy, Alaska, located in the heart of the isolated Wrangell range. A sixty-four-mile road from the highway cuts through the national park to McCarthy. Hand-operated carts hanging from a cable are the only way across the adjoining river. The town has weekly mail, no televisions, and no telephones. So what are you doing there? Gaining an in-depth understanding of Alaska's alpine zoology, botany, geology, and human ecology. The National Park Service is considering declaring this land a national wilderness area. Before it does, it wishes to study the impact of land ownership, access, level of development, and wildlife interpretation on the area. That's your job, under the supervision of a scientific team.

Length: Two months, June to July.

Fees: $1,750 covers all lodging (a.k.a. a nice tent) and meals.

Requirements: You have to be a hearty soul, comfortable sleeping outdoors and open to all sorts of unforeseen adventures, like curious elk joining you for your early morning showers or a snowfall on the Fourth of July.

Contact:
Wildland Studies
San Francisco State University
3 Mosswood Circle
Cazadero, CA 95421
707-632-5665

You Want *What?*
Negotiating for a Sabbatical

$\mathbf{W}$e start with the case of Mary Wright, so that those wanting proof that a rank-and-file employee can wheedle a sabbatical from even the most powerful and intractable of employers need look no farther. Wright, a forty-nine-year-old social-services administrator and mother of a daughter in college, works for what has to be the quintessential male-dominated, tradition-bound, top-down power structure: the Catholic archdiocese of a large midwestern city. Other bosses may *act* as if somebody died and made them pope. In the case of Wright's ultimate employer, it really happened.

Nowhere was the church's managerial style more us versus them than in its policy on sabbaticals: the priests could take them, but the nonclergical employees, such as Wright, could not. "Yet we lay people work lots of nights and lots of weekends, just as hard as the priests do," says Wright, the director of a program that gives grants to low-income communities.

Besides bristling at the general unfairness of the way

sabbaticals were divvied up, Wright had a personal stake in the matter. After a dozen years on the job, she had reached the point in her career where she didn't just want a break. She *needed* one, badly, to clear away the mental cobwebs that had accumulated from having spent much of her career looking out from behind a pencil sharpener. "My job is primarily head work; I sit at a desk and read proposals and organize people and staff committees," says Wright. "But being immersed in the poor and traveling overseas had been a passion of mine for a long, long time. I just wanted to be out of the United States for a while and learn about poverty from a different perspective, and hear and see what other people were hearing and seeing and saying about the United States and our treatment of the poor. I also really wanted to learn Spanish because I truly believe that it's going to become the second language in the United States."

But before she could take an extended break from work, she'd have to convince an organization legendary for doing things by the book to try something altogether new.

And that's indeed what she did. By the time Wright was done haggling, her boss not only granted the leave but let her take six months off with pay. Compared even to the deals offered at companies where sabbaticals are considered a basic perk of employment, Wright's sabbatical was a major coup. What's more, the precedent set by her sabbatical established a whole new policy within the archdiocese; now sabbaticals are granted to lay employees as well as to the clergy.

Far from being handed to her like a fresh box of business cards, the sabbatical was something she had to get in there and negotiate for. So, more than likely, will you. Depending on your circumstances, you may have to wrestle permission from an employer, from important clients, or from your business partners; but permission almost inevitably has to come from somebody who controls the flow of money into your pocket. After all, the person who pays you to show up on time every morning deserves—and expects—some say in whether you show up at all for the better part of a year.

Though the temptation might be great to walk away from your job and not look back, the truth is that you need to earn a living at least as much as you need to take time off. Whether you intend to go back to your old job after the sabbatical, or plan to use the references from your old job to find something new (more on this in Chapter 5), you can't afford to burn bridges. The economy being what it is these days, you can't even afford to leave them slightly scorched. The only way you can hope to leave with a RESERVED sign on your desk and keep your reputation as glowing as ever is to depart with the blessings of the people who pay your salary. How you obtain those blessings is what negotiating for a sabbatical is all about.

Unfortunately, negotiating is one of those things that we all think we should already know how to do, like ballroom dancing. Only most of us have never been shown how. So when we do it at all, we are about as inept as somebody doing the tango after having watched a couple of episodes of *The Addams Family*. Before you get around to asking for a sabbatical, there are certain negotiating steps you'll need to know if you want your request to win approval. Those steps include the following: deciding on the specifics of your proposal; doing advance research to determine the objections your boss is likely to raise; figuring out the best way to make your pitch; and coming up with fallback positions to counter your boss's objections.

GATHER INTELLIGENCE

If you remember nothing else from this chapter, remember this: information equals power. The more information you have going into the negotiations, the more formidable you'll be. Your boss may outrank you, but you can outresearch him and have an answer standing by for every argument he throws in your path—but only if you do your homework.

Don't even dare approach a superior for permission to take time off until you know the answer to the following questions:

• How indispensable are you to your organization? (The more indispensable you are, the more clout you have.)

• What's the company's official policy on sabbaticals and extended leaves of absence? How long has the policy been around? (Don't be intimidated by company policies, department rules, corporate memos, or other documents forbidding the very thing that you're about to propose. Corporate policy is often negotiable. You simply need to show why your situation is a valid exception to the rule.)

• If your company does offer sabbaticals, how long do you have to work before you're eligible for one? And how much time must pass after one sabbatical before you're eligible for another?

• When you were hired, was a sabbatical or leave of absence part of your compensation package? What were the terms of the deal? Who offered it? Was the offer put in writing?

• Does your company grant sabbaticals to some departments or people but not others? Why?

• If there's no official policy, what's the unofficial policy?

Have leaves been granted on a case-by-case basis? Under what circumstances?

• Who's the person within your company who has the power to approve your request? What's her general attitude toward encouraging professional and personal enrichment? Has she taken a sabbatical herself?

• Can you negotiate directly with the decision maker in your company, or will your immediate supervisor make your life miserable forever if you go over his head?

• To whom have leaves been granted in the past? Do they share a certain status within the company (partner, say, versus hourly employee)? Did they work for the company for a certain length of time before being granted time off? (If you're a full-time employee, you probably won't get anywhere with your sabbatical request if you've worked at the company for fewer than four years.)

• What were the terms of the sabbaticals? Were the employees kept on the payroll, allowed to keep their benefits or their seniority, and accumulate vacation and sick days? What other concessions did the company make?

• Who filled in for the employees during their hiatus? Who trained the substitutes? How was productivity affected?

• Aside from your specific company, what stance does your industry take on sabbaticals? What leave-of-absence policies do your company's closest competitors, suppliers, and clients follow?

• What's the general economic health of your company? Are layoffs impending? Are annual bonuses hefty? Are there any constraints that would make your company especially reluctant to grant your request? Are these constraints likely to worsen, making it now or never as far as your sabbatical is concerned?

• Are there crunch times during the year when your company will be especially resistant to letting you take time off? Are there slack times?

Many of these questions you can answer off the top of your head, simply from having worked for the company for a pretty good length of time. Others will take some digging. Keep your research secret until you can lay out your request for a sabbatical in an orderly manner, at just the right time and in just the right manner (a topic that will be covered later in the "Present Your Proposal" section). So where do you find the answers without announcing to the world that you want to skip town for several months? Right here:

• *The employee handbook*. Here's where you'll find the official rules on leaves of absence and sabbaticals. It's always better to read through the company's rules and regs yourself than to phone the personnel department for answers, because the employee handbook will never call up your boss and squeal.

• *Human Resources*. The usefulness of this information source all depends on the size of your company, the reputed helpfulness of the human resources or personnel department, and the odds they'll go blabbing to your boss. If you're lucky, Human Resources will be able to give you background information on whether others in the company have taken sabbaticals, what types of sabbaticals they took, and whether your situation is covered by the precedents set by those previous examples.

• *Colleagues in other departments*. You can sometimes talk more openly about your sabbatical plans with people in other departments without fear that the news will leak back to your boss, especially if you work in a large organization. The ideal person to talk to is someone who's taken a company-approved sabbatical. That person will understand your need for a sabbatical better than anybody else; she can give you the scoop on how she wangled approval from the same organization that you're about to deal with. (The next best option is simply to seek out a trustworthy friend in another department.) Most bosses hate to set precedents having to do with employee fringe benefits and other soft-and-squishy "personnel" matters, but if you can show your boss that the precedent has been set by other departments within your company, he no longer has to feel like such a bureaucratic tightrope walker.

• *Colleagues at other companies within your industry.* The best way to find out the industry standard for leaves of absence is to ask others in your industry, either contacts you know personally or industry-association reps. Again, your goal is to find precedents that will make your boss feel less alone when he grants approval for your sabbatical; if you can't find such precedents within your own company, finding them within competing organizations is the next best thing.

• *Trade publications.* Here's perhaps the easiest, most comprehensive, and most stealthful way to learn about the leave-of-absence policies practiced within your industry. Just trot down to the business reference section of your local library, and use the search terms Sabbatical, Leave of Absence, Fringe Benefit, and Vacation to look up articles on those topics in indexes that track trade publications specific to your industry. The business librarian can direct you to the best indexes for your particular occupation.

By the end of this research assignment, you should have a clear notion of the reception you're likely to receive from your boss when you ask for a sabbatical. You should know if your request will seem reasonable or if you're pushing the envelope of the company and the industry standards. If it's the latter (and there's nothing wrong with pushing the envelope; somebody's got to do it), you should also be able to put your finger on the arguments that he'll accept as justification for approving your request. Those arguments will become increasingly clear as you do your research. But what's still unclear are the particulars of the sabbatical that you intend to propose.

So far, your effort to gather intelligence has been an outward search for answers.

Now comes the time to look inward.

PRIORITIZE YOUR GOALS

Nearly all negotiations inevitably boil down to haggling over details. The last car you bought wouldn't be sitting in your garage if the sleazy dealer in the plaid slacks hadn't knocked $500 off the price and thrown in complimentary side molding and floor mats. Dealing with your boss is a lot like dealing with a used-car salesman (in case you hadn't noticed). Before you can win your boss's approval to take time off, you and she must work out the conglomeration of details that represent your vision of the perfect sabbatical— everything from when you'll depart to whether you'll draw benefits and salary.

The worst blunder you can make is to be so anxious to strike a deal that you concede on those points that represent the very heart and soul of your sabbatical. To avoid that mistake, you have to be clear about your goals right from the beginning, because you never know what concessions your boss might try to exact as early as the first meeting.

The following exercise will help you establish your goals. In the priority list below, we spell out a wide array of negotiating goals that you might like to achieve. Your task is to rank the items in terms of their importance to you. As you read the list, put the letter *A* next to those goals so critical to your happiness and success—not just in terms of your sabbatical but your life—that you'd sooner call off the sabbatical than give them up. Put *B* next to those those that would contribute to the quality of your sabbatical experience, but would still allow you to enjoy the break if you had to compromise on them. Finally, put *C* next to those items so peripheral or irrelevant to your plans that your really don't care how your boss rules on these matters.

Priority List

· You want your sabbatical to begin and end on specific dates. (If your sabbatical entails flying to Maui to witness a full solar eclipse scheduled for May 3 of next year, obviously timing is all-important, and you may have to shave some of your other demands in order to achieve this one. But if your goal is to tour the ancient cathedrals of Europe, it's not as if Notre Dame is *going* anywhere. The more flexible you can be on this crucial negotiating point, the more firm you can be on others.)

· You want the sabbatical to last a certain length of time— three months, six months, nine months, whatever—and you refuse to come back a day sooner.

· You want to receive your full salary, benefits, and bonuses during the sabbatical. (If you insist that the company fund your sabbatical, the company may want some say in how you spend your break. Is that quid pro quo something you'd really want to accept? Could you settle for partial pay and benefits in exchange for fewer demands on your time? Or would you rather finance the entire sabbatical out of savings than have work impinge on even one second of your freedom?)

• You want to make sure your absence causes no loss of productivity or profits for your company. (A noble sentiment on your part, but give it an *A* only if you mean it. Otherwise you might end up agreeing to call the office every Friday, when what you'd really rather do is stay as far away from telephone receivers as possible.)

• You want to continue accruing seniority benefits during the sabbatical. (Specifically, you'll maintain your place in the company pecking order, keep the clock running in terms of your retirement date, and as the ultimate act of chutzpah, continue to amass vacation and sick days.)

• You want to avoid all contact with your workplace during the sabbatical. (No faxes, no E-mail, nothing.)

• You want to be free of all work-related responsibilities during the sabbatical.

• You want to use some of the company's resources— WATS line, fax machine, photocopying machine, research library—to arrange your sabbatical.

• You want to handpick and/or train your replacement.

• You're unwilling to give up a raise, bonus, or vacation time in exchange for being kept on the payroll during the sabbatical.

• You want your old office (parking slot, desk, favorite chair, wide-eyed intern, or whatever) back when you return.

• You want assurances that the people who take over your duties (clients, projects) during your sabbatical will fully relinquish those duties when you return.

• You want assurances that the experiences and knowledge you gain from the sabbatical will lead to new responsibilities when you return to work.

• You want total freedom in deciding how to spend your sabbatical, without any input from your company.

Ideally, you should have a smattering of *B* and *C* items mixed in with the *As*. Now resharpen your pencil, because you're going to run through it one final time. On this last go-around, instead of ranking the items according to your priorities, you want to rank them according to your employer's (having done your research, you should be able roughly to predict her responses). Starting at the top of the list, put the letter *A* next to the negotiating goals that your boss would staunchly oppose; write *B* next to those items that she'd concede only if you could allay certain concerns; and jot down *C* next to those points that she'd readily approve.

Now take a deep breath and compare the two lists. They offer a glimpse of the negotiating turbulence to come. If you're lucky, the goals you care most about will be the very things your boss will care least about (your *A* items are her *C* items). Indeed, if your list of priorities is the exact opposite of your boss's, you'll skate through the negotiations with all your main priorities intact, and the negotiations will boil down to allaying her worries about the less-important *B* items.

The trouble comes when you and your boss care most deeply about the same two or three issues: you want to leave on March 10, and your boss needs everybody on board until the end of the tax season; you want to continue to get paid during the sabbatical, and your boss is incredulous that you'd even suggest the idea. Here's where negotiations start to resemble chess. As any grandmaster will tell you, it's almost impossible to win a game without sacrificing a few pieces. The trick is to make sure you sacrifice pawns to protect your queen, not the other way around. Because you've worked through this exercise, you should now easily be able to distinguish your highest-priority goals (the *A* items) from all the rest. If later in the negotiations you have to sacrifice some goals in order to save others, you'll know which ones to safeguard and which ones to cut.

You've now reached that point in the negotiating process where you have to leave the secretive, behind-the-scenes realm of intelligence gathering and go public with your plans. And once you go public, there's no going back.

So before you knock on your boss's door, you'd better know what you're going to say when you step inside.

PRESENT YOUR PROPOSAL

From an employer's perspective, deciding whether to let an employee take a sabbatical is a no-brainer just this side of pondering whether to put in for a transfer to the Albania office. The decision-making process barely trickles down to the level of conscious thought. Sheer bosslike instinct takes hold, and up from some reptilian part of the brain arise any number of variations on the theme of no: "Don't you realize we've had our worst third quarter in a decade?" "Do you see *me* taking any vacations around here?" The list goes on.

During this first meeting with your boss, countering those objections isn't enough. You have to keep the objections from taking form in the first place. If you can steer your sabbatical proposal around this initial seizure of defensiveness and negativity, if you can make your boss actually think about your proposal rather than just react to it, you stand an excellent chance of going the distance. To achieve that objective, you want to pick the right time, the right place, and the right tone.

Choose the Right Time

One of the best ways to take the gasp factor out of your request for a sabbatical is to let your boss have plenty of warning that you'll be leaving. The further in advance you give notice, the likelier your boss will sign off on the deal. An early announcement will also go a long way toward convincing your boss that the sabbatical is a means of achieving important professional and personal goals, not merely some flighty, midlife-crisis whim. "You should ask for permission as far in advance as possible," says Ed Warnock, a Pacific Northwest–based management consultant who helps businesspeople hone their negotiation skills. "If you know you want to go to Europe and study art, it would be far less threatening to your supervisor if you said, 'Sometime in the next five years . . .' than if you said, 'Sometime between September and Christmas I want to take off sixty days.' Supervisors panic when they hear stuff like that."

Both you and your boss will need plenty of lead time to prepare for your absence so that the sabbatical doesn't unduly disrupt the status quo. A good rule of thumb is, give your boss at least one month's notice (two is even better) for every month that you wish to take off. If you want six months off, inform your boss at least six months in advance. Violate that rule, and you may have to make all sorts of unattractive promises—that you'll call in to the office once a week to put out fires, you'll take work with you on the trip. After all, somebody has to make sure productivity doesn't suffer in your absence, and that somebody will probably end up being you. (Note this exception: if your initial research reveals that an early announcement may turn you into a sitting duck should layoffs occur, shrink the length of your notice as much as you comfortably can. By keeping quiet, you'll maintain a low profile during the next round of layoffs, and with any luck, the purge will be over by the time you're ready to let people know about your plans. Even if you get booted later on, you'll have delayed the inevitable until just shortly before you were planning to leave voluntarily.)

What if a trip to the other side of the world suddenly presents itself out of nowhere, and you have to decide soon whether to do it—so soon that you can't give much advance warning? First, give as much notice as possible. One month is still better than one week. And second, be upfront about the iffyness of your plans. More than likely, if an opportunity has sprung itself on you as fast as all that, you're probably still wrestling with the question of whether you'll be able to go, anyway. Let your boss know this. He won't feel as threatened by a proposal that's only in the possibility stage.

When James Nelson found out about the Eisenhower Exchange Fellowship, a program that sends Americans abroad to work with their counterparts in other countries, this Mississippi assistant secretary of state instantly became intrigued with the idea, but had only two months to apply. The short deadline precluded any advance warning. But when meeting with the boss to broach the idea, Nelson took some of the sting out the news by emphasizing that he might not be accepted into this highly competitive program. " 'I don't have a chance in hell of getting this,' I told him, 'but if I do, I just want you to know that . . . I'm going! It's a once-in-a-lifetime experience and you can fire me or whatever, but I'm going,' " says Nelson, who'd always had a friendly relationship with his employer. "He was very supportive and just as excited as I was."

Choose the Right Place

Look at the situation from a boss's perspective, and you can see why the first few minutes of the negotiations are often the most crucial. Imagine how you'd feel if one of your employees cornered you in the hall one morning and insisted that you hold open his job until he wrapped up his pleasure trip to Singapore, which, by the way, should conclude about eight months from now. The guy isn't asking for vacation time that's coming due; he's talking about something else entirely. For all you know, he's already been chattering about his plans to coworkers, and this strange notion has spread through the rest of the department at the speed of gossip. Suddenly the team that you've spent the past five years assembling is threatening to break apart like floor joists in an earthquake. To keep your boss from feeling caught off guard, never buttonhole him in the elevator with your proposal. Instead, make an appointment to meet with him in his office or over lunch. Make sure you've both dedicated at least a half-hour to the meeting.

Choose the Right Tone

Need we state that ultimatums almost never work in these situations? Nor does slamming your fist on the desk. Nor, for that matter, does acting whiny, making cynical asides at staff meetings, or jumping up on a table in a Norma Rae show of solidarity with organized labor everywhere. Your boss has enough hassles in his life and doesn't need another one. You'll only turn him into an adversary instead of an ally if you try to browbeat him into acceding to your demands. In fact, don't demand; propose, as in, "I'd like to recommend that . . ." "I'd like to propose that . . ." Begin with the phase,

"This is what I have in mind," and reel off your main points. Encourage an attitude of mutual brainstorming. Your boss will feel a greater sense of ownership in the deal if you invite him to help you fine-tune the proposal.

One hot-button word to avoid when talking with your boss about a sabbatical is the word *sabbatical*. It's a terrific, romantic, adventurous way to describe your journey to the outside world, but it's not the right word to use with your boss, because it smacks of entitlement. "*Sabbatical* sets human resources people on edge because the word suggests that if you're here for six years, we'll give you the seventh year off," says Martha Peak, an editor at the American Management Association.

Peak ought to know. She recently became the first person in her organization to receive a leave of absence for a reason other than pregnancy. For years, she and her husband had been planning to relocate from New York City to a small town in Maine. To earn a living in rural New England, she fulfilled all the requirements for a master's degree in teaching—with one exception. She still needed to take four months off from work to complete the student-teaching portion of the curriculum. She attributes her success in negotiating those four months off in part to the fact that she steered clear of using the word *sabbatical* during her discussions with company decision makers, choosing instead the more benign term *leave of absence*. "There's this 'you owe me' thing attached to *sabbatical*," she says, "that can really alienate employers."

Now comes the time to craft the first draft of a written proposal that spells out your goals while simultaneously soothing your boss's concerns. This document isn't something you should show your boss—at least not initially. You wouldn't want to suggest you've already figured out the details of your sabbatical and all you need from your boss is his initials. He'll feel that he has only two options: to accept or to reject the proposal outright.

Instead, the best way to raise the subject of the sabbatical is in the format of a one-on-one meeting. The great thing about direct dialogue is that you can instantly gauge your boss's reaction; if he recoils at one particular part of the proposal, you can immediately backpedal and downplay its importance. Conversations are fluid; the written word is fixed and inflexible. (The one time when it's better to show up at every meeting armed with a written proposal is when company protocol mandates that you negotiate with your immediate supervisor, when really it's somebody higher on the organizational chart who'll make the final decision. This situation is always awkward, because intermediaries tend to twist and tangle your message and infuse it with their own agenda. The way you keep their influence to a minimum is to state your case in writing, thereby transforming your immediate supervisor's role from that of propaganda minister to errand boy.)

So then why bother to actually have a draft proposal on paper? During the meeting with your boss, you'll need to state your case in an orderly, persuasive manner, and there's no better way to organize your thoughts than to put them down on paper. After you and your boss have that first talk face to face, you'll need to follow up the conversation with a memo summarizing all the points you spelled out during the meeting. The written proposal that you're about to prepare will essentially be that memo—with some last-minute editing thrown in to reflect the "hot spots" you may have hit during the initial meeting.

As you write your proposal, be sure it addresses the following questions:

Why Do You Want to Take a Sabbatical?

The most powerful reason is one that has some work-related connection: you'll gain useful skills or important business contacts; you'll be adding wealth to the company's knowledge bank. Just don't strain the bounds of credulity in talking up the benefits to your employer. Don't insist, for instance, that you'll get twice as much work done on that sailboat as you would at your desk, since you'll be taking all your files along on the cruise. Bosses aren't that stupid. Even *stupid* bosses aren't that stupid.

You can make a legitimate argument that the sabbatical will benefit the company if you can answer yes to any of the following questions: (1) Will your sabbatical expand your mastery of another language or another culture? (2) Will it let you gain new skills, or sharpen old ones? (3) Will you be learning things that could lend new insights into the way your company does business? (4) Will you be traveling to places where your company might open up new markets? (5) Will you be meeting people who'll be welcome additions to your office Rolodex? (6) Will your absence allow other people in your department to assume some of your duties, thereby broadening their skills and letting them have a taste of new responsibilities? To win over the archdiocese, social-services administrator Mary Wright talked about how she planned on taking intensive Spanish-language training, which would make her better able to help the church meet the needs of the growing Hispanic community.

While the work-related argument packs the most punch, bosses can also be swayed by other reasons that have nothing to do with boosting the company's bottom line. The most persuasive are these: charitable works (it's hard to turn down an employee's request to do good in the world, especially if the company exhibits more than a glimmer of social conscience); family matters, such as taking your kids on a family-history tour of the United States, before they turn into jaded teenagers; a once-in-a-lifetime experience, such as traveling with an environmental group to South America to study nearly extinct tree frogs; a broadened perspective (having done the same job for umpteen years, you need a break to clear your head, recharge your batteries, and expand your horizons, and when you come back, you'll be more of a go-getter than ever). If your reason for taking a sabbatical doesn't fit neatly into one of those boxes, try to wedge it in there anyway.

Why Now?

Typically, the timing issue hinges on the current financial health of your company. If you work for a highly successful firm, your boss needs all hands on deck to get the burgeoning workload accomplished, and her chief objection to your taking a sabbatical may be that she simply can't afford to lose a single warm body. To allay that objection, you need to line up somebody else to take your place, so that your absence doesn't interject so much as a hiccup into the company's meteoric growth projections. In your favor is the fact that companies flush with success tend to be brimming with subordinates eager to assume greater responsibility, and their professional advancement is key to the company's immediate benefit.

If you work for a stable company that plods along from year to year without any major changes good or bad, the biggest objection that you're likely to run into is the argument, "We've just never done this sort of thing before." Stable companies tend to be places that attract creatures of habit, and the best way of responding to that mind-set is to make the most of the company's predictability. If things around the office are as unchanging as all that, the company's peak periods and slack times should be well established. Therefore, arrange your sabbatical to correspond with the slow periods, and nobody can argue that the place will fall apart if you aren't around to hold it together.

If the company is caught in a financial death spiral, or simply an anemic period of decline marked by cost-cutting, layoffs, and company-picnic cancellations, you're likely to confront the objection of, "How can we possibly let you take an extended vacation when we're having to lay people off?" Your response depends on how badly you want to remain at the company, and whether you're likely to be among the permanently jettisoned in the not-too-distant future.

One option, assuming your job isn't long for this world anyway, is to step forward and volunteer to be laid off in exchange for a severance package that will fund your sabbatical. Why would a company agree to such a deal? Simply to avoid the trauma of having to involuntarily lay off some other poor slob who needs every last paycheck to keep his kids in diapers. Another option, assuming your job is reasonably secure and you want to return to it after the sabbatical ends, is to request a leave of absence at reduced pay, thereby giving the company some financial breathing room until the hard times subside. Essentially, the company is a foundering life raft, and you're volunteering to tread water for a while, thereby buying time for everybody else. Your motives may not be entirely altruistic, but in the eyes of your company, you're a hero. *Bon voyage.*

What Steps Will You Take to Ensure That the Company Benefits from the Sabbatical—or at the Very Least, Isn't Inconvenienced?

Your boss will want to hear about how you—not he—will make sure that office productivity doesn't flag during your absence. Who'll do the work? Who'll train your replacements to do the work? Who'll do their work while they're doing yours? You'll lose credibility fast if you fail to talk in specifics.

Whenever possible, point out that the purpose of your leave of absence fits right in with some larger, overarching mission of the company. In some organizations, employee morale and personal growth—two very good reasons for taking a sabbatical—rank high on the organization's list of priorities. You know company culture is with you if the employee manual reads like the human resources equivalent of the Swedish constitution, promising educational grants, child-care centers, job sharing, flex time, and wellness programs as part of the basic benefits package. Even at small companies, bosses often go out of their way to raise the quality of life for their employees by letting workers knock off early in order to take classes at the local community college or adjust their hours to be home in time to meet the kids' school bus. In asking for a sabbatical, you're really just tapping into the corporate generosity that's already there. Point out that fact in your proposal, and you'll have considerable clout on your side.

What worked in New York City–based editor Martha Peak's favor, in fact, was that the purpose of her sabbatical—completing her master's in teaching—dovetailed with her company's emphasis on education and self-improvement. Says Peak: "This is not some cutthroat organization where a woman who goes off on the mommy track for a while is considered a second-class worker. Therefore, if I want to get my teaching degree, if I want to get my MBA or my pilot's license, there's a corporate culture around here that says, 'Gee, good for her.' "

Likewise, in her dealings with the Catholic archdiocese, social-services administrator Mary Wright pointed out that she wanted to travel to Latin America and learn firsthand about the people whom her proverty programs were trying to help. For that reason, she argued, her proposal fell right in line with the recommendations summed up in a recent report by U.S. Catholic bishops, a report that stated, "We call on our leaders and fellow citizens to demonstrate creativity and determination in building institutions which will assure the world community a more just, peaceful, and sustainable future." Wright even typed up that section of the report and included it with the written request that she gave to her boss. Short of stapling a handwritten endorsement from the pope to her proposal, she couldn't have been any clearer about showing the link between the goals of her sabbatical and the goals of the church.

Why Should You Receive the Sabbatical Rather Than Someone Else in the Company?

This is basically the "Who do you think you are?" issue that needs to be resolved, so that your boss has something to say when other employees barge through her door and make a similar request. Have you worked at the company for a considerable length of time? Have you come through in some special way for the company? Are you an indispensable member of the organization—meaning, would the lights go off tomorrow if you tendered your resignation? Don't pat yourself on the back to an obnoxious degree, but you should subtly suggest that you've paid your dues and now you need a break. Your true clout, in fact, lies in your reputation as a valued employee. If you're a key player in your company (as defined by your role in directly making or saving money for the company), or if you can show that the sabbatical will directly benefit the company, you stand a good chance of receiving not just a sabbatical but a paid sabbatical. With benefits. And the promise that your job will be secure until you return. And the assurance that you'll be able to put the knowledge you gained during the sabbatical to good use when you come back. If you aren't such a key player, you may have to settle for an unpaid sabbatical and see how far your boss will go toward kicking in at least partial benefits. If you've been a lackluster performer who's barely survived your last three review sessions, you stand about as much chance of getting a paid sabbatical as you do of convincing a total stranger to cosign your car loan. In fact, if your boss has been thinking about getting rid of you anyway, your request for a sabbatical might be just the excuse she's been waiting for to tell you to take a hike—permanently. For this reason, it's a good idea to raise the issue of a sabbatical only if you have some sense that your boss thinks highly of your work and would want to do everything reasonable to keep you happy.

Assuming you've built up a strong track record, bosses (and clients, if you happen to be self-employed) can sometimes let loose with a surprising tide of support and best wishes when you announce your plans for a sabbatical. Milton Stewart, a partner with the prestigious Pacific Northwest law firm Davis, Wright, Tremaine, had anticipated fist-shaking objections from important clients when they heard he was taking three months off to travel through Europe with his wife. He received heartfelt congratulations instead. "One of the things that I found was that my clients didn't just think that I was a good lawyer, but that they cared about me as a person. I think all of them envied me, but in a very positive way. Many, many said, 'You know, that's something I've always hoped to do.' And almost all of them genuinely wished me well and were pleased for me."

What Details of the Sabbatical Require Your Boss's Approval?

At the initial meeting, it's best not to overwhelm your boss with too many details at once. It's better to leave some questions unanswered and let your boss help you create the plan. It will give your boss some ownership in it, which will help her support the sabbatical more strongly when she has to sell it to her bosses. Mainly bring up the date when you'd like to leave, the length of time you'd like to be away, and perhaps one or two other items. The remaining priorities you and she can hammer out at subsequent meetings, after she's warmed up to the general concept of giving you the time off. Once the details have been worked out—a process that might take several meetings—you'll fire off one final memo summarizing every piece of the agreement.

Of course, your proposal will draw so heavily from the details of your life and work history that there's no way you can simply take a generic script from this book and change a few pronouns to make it read like yours. Consequently, the following example won't match your situation exactly, but it will at least give you a pattern to follow in shaping your own proposal.

> *Dear Mona,*
> As you know, I've often talked about my interest in bicycling. Well, a rare opportunity has come my way to pedal through Europe—Barcelona to Moscow, to be

exact—with several other serious cyclists. The trip will last from April 1st to October 20th of next year. I very much would like to fulfill this lifelong dream of mine. What makes the trip especially attractive is its timing: my departure would take place immediately after our department completes the fall-winter development projects.

I see this trip as a once-in-a-lifetime opportunity to challenge myself athletically, to broaden my knowledge of the world, and to return to work six months later with a fresh perspective and renewed energy and enthusiasm. Having worked here now for six years, and having worked hard to help make numerous development projects a success, I firmly believe that this leave of absence will expand my understanding of other cultures in ways that will at least indirectly contribute to the knowledge that I bring to my job. Staffers have always been encouraged here to pursue educational goals; indeed, the company even offers financial help for that purpose. While the trip I'm proposing doesn't meet the definition of formal education, I'm certain that the journey across Europe will be every bit as intellectually stimulating as anything I could experience in a classroom.

The leave of absence would begin in mid-spring, when we customarily wrap up our development cycle. Because the trip won't actually start for more than seven months from now, I have plenty of time to bring Jerry and Lisa up to speed. Both have mentioned to me on several occasions that they'd like to assume greater responsibility, and my leave of absence would give them that chance. In addition, I should mention that my absence will span the summer months, when we normally have college interns helping out in the office, so Jerry and Lisa will have assistants who can lend a hand.

To sum up, I'd like to request a personal leave of absence starting on April 1st and ending on October 20th. Prior to my departure, I'll take full responsibility for training Jerry and Lisa to carry out my duties while I'm away. I also plan to make sure that the preliminary research reports on the next round of development projects are well under way by the date of my departure. I would also like to work out an arrangement whereby I would still receive my salary and benefits during the leave. Since it's highly likely that at least one new development project will get the go-ahead during my absence, the responsibility for launching the project can remain with Jerry and Lisa, and by then, I'll be back to handle the new development projects coming on board.

Thank you for considering this proposal, and as we agreed, I look forward to meeting with you again on Thursday at 2 P.M. to discuss the details further.

Thanks,
Victoria

FEND OFF COUNTERARGUMENTS

No matter how cogently you present the proposal, be prepared to swim against a hard current of objections. Here's where the discussions can all too easily escalate into a battle of wills. Given that you have less authority than your boss, the odds are a virtual certainty that the loser would be you. Therefore, your goal is to avoid a confrontation altogether, and instead work toward turning your boss from adversary to ally. To do that, you need to respond to each objection in ways that demonstrate your loyalty and concern for the company, without being so conciliatory that you gut your sabbatical.

Fortunately, bosses usually spout off the same half-dozen objections over and over, so predicting what their arguments will be is about as easy as predicting whether it will rain some time this year in Seattle. Here are the objections you can expect from your employers, and the responses you should counter with:

OBJECTION #1: "I don't want to be bothered training someone else to do your job."

YOUR ANSWER IS: "I'm going to find and train somebody else who will take over my duties while I'm gone."

But be prepared to back it up with specifics. Whom do you have in mind as a replacement? How did other departments in your company handle similar situations? These are questions you need to hash out in advance of meeting with your boss. Indeed, if you leave this chore to your boss, he's liable to choose the path of least resistance—which would be to deny your request for your sabbatical and preserve the status quo.

OBJECTION #2: "If I let you take a sabbatical, the rest of the staff will want one, too."

YOUR ANSWER IS: "If it works in the end for both me and the company, it might be a win-win situation that could work for other employees, too. What's wrong with that?"

This objection underscores your boss's very real concern about setting a bad precedent. The way you calm him down is by making it clear that you're seeking approval for only the specific framework of your proposal. You're asking not for an extended vacation but for an opportunity to do something that will benefit both you and the company. You can also argue that your proposal deserves special consideration because of the uniquely urgent nature of your plans. Maybe you want to tour Vietnam before other American companies have a chance to gain a foothold. Maybe you want to take the last tramp steamer around South America before it stops running altogether. The time-sensitive nature of your sabbatical—whatever it might be—will establish that you're asking for the chance to do something that can never be done again, not merely the chance to do a longer version of your usual summer vacation.

OBJECTION #3: "You're going to inconvenience other people."

YOUR ANSWER IS: "No, let me show you the plan. No one will be inconvenienced."

Getting someone else up to speed on how to cover for you is one of those chores that's easy to put off until the last minute. Bosses know this, and they're never going to approve a sabbatical until you can make the convincing case that your departure will create no more than a ripple in the smooth running of the department. Magazine editor Martha Peak took this duty so seriously that she incorporated it into her performance plan—the list of objectives by which employees are judged at their annual review. To offset any disruption caused by her absence, she wrote all the magazine editorials through May of the following year and assigned all the stories in advance. She designated a senior copy editor to become acting managing editor; this person's job would be to run the magazine on a day-to-day basis.

She appointed another editor to handle staffing and budget problems. "I haven't seen any groans from either of them," says Peak. "If they're smart—and they are—they'll take this experience, stick it on their résumé, and use it as a feather in their cap."

OBJECTION #4: "How can I be sure you're going to come back?"

YOUR ANSWER IS: "I'll guarantee you I'll come back, if you'll guarantee me there'll be a place to come back to."

The credibility of your answer ultimately depends on whether you've built up a trusting relationship with your boss. Trust is based on your track record, on whether your past actions bespeak reliability and credibility. One way to convince people that you do indeed intend to return to your job is to start talking about your sabbatical well in advance of when it actually begins. That way, your boss not only has a chance to get used to the idea but also can see where the sabbatical fits into the overall direction of your career.

OBJECTION #5: "Why should the company keep paying your salary and benefits just so you can take an extended vacation?"

YOUR ANSWER: "Because it isn't just a vacation. I'm going to do things that will help the company."

Even if you need a sabbatical to get away from work, you'll be strengthening your negotiating hand mightily if you sprinkle activities into your sabbatical that will somehow benefit your boss. Spend time learning the foreign language spoken by one of your company's major suppliers. Point out to your boss that you'll come back so refreshed and rejuvenated that you'll probably get more done despite taking three months off than if you'd stayed at your desk all year. Mention that other companies in your industry are offering leaves of absence (if, in fact, they are), and if your company wants to stay competitive in hiring the best employees, it also needs to be competitive in its compensation package. The point is, the more connections you can make between your sabbatical and the success of the company, the likelier a paid sabbatical will be approved.

OBJECTION #6: "Nothing like this has ever been approved before."
YOUR ANSWER: "Actually, it has."

If your boss raises the "we've never done this sort of thing before" objection, you know you're dealing with someone who's been soaking in the bureaucratic Jacuzzi a little too long, and bureaucrats are deathly fearful of setting precedents of any kind. If you've done your homework, you should be able to cite examples either from your company or from similar companies where employees have been granted leaves of absences.

This, in fact, is how Mary Wright made the Catholic archdiocese take her demands for a sabbatical more seriously. Says Wright: "Whenever I would bring up the issue of a sabbatical, my boss just kept saying, 'I don't know.' There was no such thing as sabbaticals for laypeople in the archdiocese. So I just started calling around to other churches to find out how they dealt with sabbaticals. One of my very, very dear friends works for the Lutheran church. She had just finished a sabbatical, so I used the argument that she does basically the same work for the Lutherans that I do for the Catholics. I've been here for twelve years; she got a sabbatical after seven years. I pulled all the information together into a written proposal for my boss, and said, 'This is what the other denominations are doing. This is what the business world does. Here is a written proposal for what I want, what I think is fair and just for me.' "

The fact that she cited other denominations in her report apparently struck an ecclesiastical nerve. "He took my report and read it through and said, 'Let me think about this for a while,' " says Wright.

And indeed he did. After more prodding from Wright, her boss granted the request.

HAMMER OUT THE SPECIFICS

If the first meeting was basically about gently introducing your boss to the concept of sabbaticals, the subsequent meetings are about fleshing out your proposal with details. Here's where you talk money, dates, benefits, seniority status, parking-slot privileges. Almost all negotiations involve some give-and-take, if for no other reason than that your boss won't want to seem like a total pushover. More than likely, in fact, your boss will have legitimate gripes about some details of your proposal; perhaps they threaten to hamper productivity, perhaps they run counter to chiseled-in-stone company policy, or perhaps they simply might lead to howls of protest from jealous colleagues. Either way, you need to be prepared for some serious rounds of haggling. This is a business deal you're trying to strike with your boss. You want him to give you a sabbatical, and it's your job to find out the price you'll pay. Do you simply need to be a reliable, dedicated employee? Do you need to work nights and weekends for the next year in order to win approval? What's the price?

It's during this dickering phase of negotiations that many proposals die an ugly death. It happens because people invest so much of their ego in fighting for one piece of the proposal—and it may not even be a crucial piece—that they can't bear the thought of compromising it even a little bit. Here's where the priority list you drew up earlier in the chapter will be invaluable. It not only provides you with an inventory of the details that need to be discussed but if your boss demands concessions, it also shows you where to cut back your proposal without doing significant damage to your sabbatical.

Let's go over some negotiating ground rules to improve your odds during the haggling process:

1. *Ask for everything.* Literally every item that you consider a priority—even a low priority—should be placed on the bargaining table. If you don't ask, you'll never give your boss the opportunity to say yes. Indeed, despite your best efforts to research your boss's responses in advance, you can never be sure of the reaction you'll get to various parts of your proposal. Asking that your salary remain in force during the sabbatical might seem to you an impossible demand. But perhaps from your boss's perspective she'd gladly keep you on the payroll during the sabbatical if you'd only agree to postpone your trip until the following year. You want to use the company phone after hours to line up your travel plans? You want to move back into your old office when the sabbatical ends? You want to stay on the dental plan? Ask. Write down everything you want to ask for, and take the list in with you to the meeting. Too often, people fail to ask for things either because they want to avoid confrontations or because they simply forget. Don't fret, and don't forget. Ask.

2. *Don't jabber with colleagues.* Never let coworkers

know ahead of time about the negotiations, because you'll only end up making them jealous, and they'll respond either with petty acts of contempt directed at you or storm the boss's office asking for equal treatment. Let colleagues know about your plans only after the deal has been completed.

3. *Use your lower priority goals as cannon fodder.* When concessions need to be made, start with the items lowest on your list. If any of your lower priority goals happen to rank high on your boss's list of priorities, you'll knock the steam out of his obstinacy in a hurry if those are the items that you compromise on first.

4. *Be a problem solver.* Before you compromise, search for win-win alternatives that will make both parties happy. Let's say, for example, that you want your sabbatical to begin on April 1, but your boss wants you to stick around until at least June 1. Before you capitulate, find out why he wants you to delay your trip. Does a special project need to be completed before your departure? If so, could you finish the tasks before April 1 by working weekends or handing off other responsibilities to someone else? If you can eliminate the dilemma that lies at the core of your boss's objection, you'll also eliminate the objection.

5. *Don't sacrifice too much too soon.* Let's again assume that you want the sabbatical to last for six months, and your boss is insistent on two months. Rather than give in completely, try to settle on a time frame in between. As you haggle back and forth, however, squelch the temptation to suggest that you and your boss split the difference and settle on four months off. The problem with "splitting the difference" is that you instantly give away half the battleground to your opponent. If your boss then hangs tough by still insisting on two months, you'll both be tussling over whether the break will be two or three months if you naively offer to split

the difference again. When you agree to ratchet back your position, it's far better to do so incrementally. If your opening proposal is six months, for instance, make your next offer five and a half months. That way, you'll boost the possibility that the final agreed-upon length of the break will be far closer to six months than to two.

6. *Give yourself time to think.* If your boss comes back with a counteroffer, don't feel that you have to instantly accept or reject it. Most people need time to ponder new information. Instead of blurting out a response that you might later regret, simply say, "I'd like to think this over, and I'll get back to you in a day or two." Now go home and literally sleep on the offer. Let the emotional roller-coaster circling through your brain come to a stop, and weigh the pros and cons dispassionately.

7. *Be creative about compensation strategies.* If there's an area where your problem-solving skills need to be at their sharpest, it's in the area of compensation. Naturally, you'd like to keep your salary and benefits in effect during the sabbatical, and naturally, your boss would rather turn off the money faucet entirely. Given this dilemma, how do you fund your sabbatical? For starters, you can do like the Canadians, and earmark a portion of your current salary to be set aside until such time as you take your sabbatical. Thanks to a 1988 revision in Canada's Income Tax Act, employees in that country can defer a percentage of their salary to finance what would otherwise be an unpaid leave of absence, from six months to a year in length. The employer stashes the deferred salary in an interest-bearing account where it remains tax-free until withdrawn. Granted, Americans can't avail themselves of the tax benefits enjoyed by Canadians, but the idea of slowly but steadily contributing each month to a sabbatical fund makes sense no matter what side of the border you

live on. Arrange with your bank to have a certain amount of money deducted from your checking account every month and placed in an interest-bearing savings account.

Another good salary-stretching alternative is to tell your boss that you'll pass up your next raise, bonus, or vacation in exchange for remaining on the payroll during part or all of your sabbatical. (This option only makes sense, however, if there's little or no chance that you'll lose your job anytime soon; otherwise, you could be sacrificing current income with no hope of ever getting it back.) If the point of contention is whether the company should continue to provide you with health insurance during the sabbatical, remember this: you need medical coverage just as much when you're not working as when you are, and generally the best deal in town is the insurance you already receive from your employer. In fact, not only is health insurance expensive when you go out and buy it on your own, but insurance companies in some parts of the country won't even sell you long-term coverage—at least not without a lot of stipulations—if you're in anything but the best of health. For that reason, you should bargain heavily to keep your company policy. Even if you have to offer to pay part of your medical insurance costs during the sabbatical in exchange for your boss's agreeing to keep you on the company policy, you'd still be ahead in most cases by doing so.

8. *Keep written records.* Take a notepad into the negotiations, and jot down all offers and counteroffers. Nobody's memory is perfect, and as the negotiations progress, you'll want to be able to refer back to what's already been decided upon. When the negotiations have been concluded, type up the final deal in the form of a memo and send a copy to your boss. This way, both you and she will have a copy of the agreement in your files, and when you return to work six

months or a year later, there will be no confusion about the terms that had been reached.

Your memo should read something like this:

To: Mona
From: Victoria

This memo pulls together my understanding of information discussed formally and informally with you during the past months.

I will be taking a leave of absence from April 1st to October 20th of next year. I will have 19 days of accrued paid vacation time, which will be applied to the first part of my leave. During the remainder of my leave, I will draw half salary. That is a very generous offer, and I appreciate the confidence in me that it represents. I am also pleased that the company will keep my medical benefits intact during my leave of absence. I understand that my obligation is to continue to copay at my current rate.

Prior to April 1st, I will be responsible for meeting all my usual deadlines, plus those projects scheduled through June 1st. I understand that I will be expected to contact Jerry and Lisa by telephone once every two weeks during the first month of the leave of absence, in order to make myself available for questions. They will share responsibilities for handling the duties I normally perform. Grace and J. T. will also be available to assist, along with the summer intern, whom I will select before my departure. Before leaving, I will also leave a detailed message on my voice mail, providing information as to whom people should call for appropriate reasons.

In recognition of their greater responsibility, both

Jerry and Lisa will be promoted to assistant editors. They—along with Grace and J. T.—will report to Mike during my absence. Upon my return, I will resume my duties as their immediate supervisor. My title will be unaffected by this leave of absence, and my duties afterward will remain unchanged.

Many thanks as always for your continued support.

9. *The last resort: consider quitting.* Suppose you can't take the sting out of your boss's demands, despite your efforts at negotiating a mutually satisfactory sabbatical. Suppose, for example, he insists that you stay in close contact with the office throughout the sabbatical, but you consider it too much of an intrusion. The choice is this: do you accept the sabbatical according to the terms he's offering, do you call the whole thing off, or do you quit?

The answer is spelled out right there on your priority list. For some folks, the sabbatical really does outrank their job, and they'd rather be unemployed if that's the only way to take some time off. Such was the case with Jean Bone, a Seattle social worker who'd long dreamed of hiking the Pacific Crest Trail. But when she asked her boss for six months off to do the trek, her boss would grant only a three-month sabbatical. Bone responded by quitting and doing the hike anyway. But the important thing was, she didn't storm out of the office in a huff. She and her employer parted on good terms, and when Bone finished the trek, she was rehired by the same organization.

Without a doubt, quitting is a drastic last step, but if you do it, do it well. Treat your boss with respect throughout the negotiations. Let it be known that your resignation doesn't represent any sort of ultimatum; rather, it shows the fact that at this stage of your life, you really need to take time off to pursue other very important goals. Don't get snippy. Don't vent your long-buried opinions regarding your boss's obsessive-compulsive personality. Even if you can't wait to escape this private hellhole, remember that your negative attitudes may spring as much from burnout as from any realistic appraisal of the working conditions. A year from now, when your stress level has dropped down off the Richter scale, your old workplace may seem like a pretty decent place, after all. Even if you don't go back, you'll probably still need references. The best way to leave both options open is to be polite and professional in every way possible.

KEEP NEGOTIATING

Before you do anything as irrevocable as quitting, you should be aware that there's one other thing you can do. *You can negotiate to keep negotiating.* With time as your ally, you can keep the discussions bubbling along indefinitely, in hopes that your boss will cave in before you do. Granted, this tactic requires patience. But the negotiation process isn't something that can be rushed when you're up against an employer who can shut down the talks at any moment and walk away from the table. "Say to your boss, 'Okay, let's let it lie for now. When's a good time to bring it up again?' " advises negotiations expert Ed Warnock. "If he says, 'In six months,' go write down on your calendar six months from now, 'Bring up sabbatical.' "

This, in fact, was the tactic that Mary Wright—the social-services administrator who hoped to travel abroad and learn Spanish—used in her dealings with the archdiocese: sheer doggedness. A few months after she'd received permission to take the sabbatical, word came down from the top that the archdiocese was strapped for cash and needed to eliminate all unnecessary expenses. Given the severity of the financial crunch, Wright's sabbatical was canceled.

Now, consider the predicament from Wright's viewpoint. She'd previously been told that she could go. She'd already found a place to live in Latin America. She'd settled on a charitable organization that she wanted to work with there. She'd gone out of her way to arrange things so that her daughter, who was in high school at the time, could join her there as well. She was a packed suitcase away from leaving, and suddenly the whole trip was called off.

But she wanted the sabbatical too much to let it slip away. She decided to hang tough. "Although my boss had already approved my sabbatical, he came to me and said, 'I don't know that we can do this,' " says Wright. "And I said, 'Absolutely. How can you send me off on a paid sabbatical when the archdiocese is cutting budgets and cutting staff?' I told him, 'I'm going to let this drop, but I want you to know I'm coming back next year with this same request.' " And that's exactly what she did: a year later, she went back to her boss and pitched the proposal all over again. This time, the church was in better financial shape. And this time, Wright came away with the answer that she'd been waiting for.

"The Chinese have a saying: 'The person who returns from a journey is never quite the same person who began it,' " says Wright. "I totally agree. I'm an extrovert by nature, but I found my introverted side while I was on sabbatical. Not only did I find it but I was pleased with it. I remember sitting on a beach in Nicaragua, just observing everything around me, and letting go of absolutely everything. Every cell of my body was open to what I was smelling and tasting and seeing and feeling at that moment. It wasn't like it is in the U.S., where we're always filling our lives with so much that we can never just enjoy a puddle, never just enjoy a rainbow. I found myself really able to do those things while I was away. I loved it so much, I'm ready to leave again. I'm not sure when. But I know it will happen."

More important, she knows how to make it happen.

And now, so do you.

How to Use a Break to Jump-Start Your Career

Do you absolutely adore your job and hope for nothing more in life? Then jump to the next chapter. But if you're interested in using your sabbatical as a way to change to a new job or improve the one you have now, then consider these two strategies: (1) analyze what job or promotion you want when you return, and (2) lay the groundwork for that outcome both before and while you're gone.

It worked for Jennifer Grant. "When I was a trader, I felt like I was being crammed into shoes that didn't fit," says Grant, who left Wall Street to spend a year fulfilling her fantasy of being a ski bum on the slopes of Aspen, Colorado. "Trading was a very stressful, numbers-oriented job, and even though I was making a lot of money, I knew it wasn't the right field for me. In Aspen, I did a lot of soul-searching about what was important to me." During her hours on the slopes, she met new people everywhere she went. And she asked them all about their jobs. "I started to realize that I was not good at banking and that my natural strength was dealing with people." Grant moved from working on the trading floor pricing securities—an occupation for the mathematically inclined—to being an investment banker/headhunter who calls fifty or sixty people a day. "I feel great about my job now," she says.

Like Grant, you might use a sabbatical as a way to leap to a new career or reshape your present one. Maybe you've reached a career junction where you're not sure whether you want to continue with your present work. Or maybe you just want to reshape your present job—but you're at a loss as to how to start. Here's how.

KEEP THE FUTURE IN MIND

There's a painless, intriguing way to keep a link with the working world while having the time of your life: do everything you want on your sabbatical, but present it to the outside world as a smart business move. That doesn't mean your sabbatical days must be filled with thoughts of work. It merely means that work has to be taken into account. Look at this as a long-term investment strategy. You don't have to check on those investments all the time, but you do need to look at the quarterly statements. In a similar fashion, you need to periodically think of the future while you're reveling in the present.

How Will It Look on Your Résumé?

When first shaping your sabbatical plans, think for a second about how you'd explain it later to a future employer or your coworkers. Does it make for a good story? Or does it sound a little, well, dubious? Or—and this is even more telling—

imagine yourself reading the résumé of a sabbatical taker. What would make you utter "what a jerk" under your breath and what would leave you with admiration and low-grade envy for the person? Sometimes it's just in the wording, sometimes it means picking a sabbatical that hits a certain chord with people.

Nuclear engineer Brian Booth chose to hike the 2,600-mile Pacific Crest Trail for two reasons: he wanted an ambitious hiking trip, and he wanted an achievement the outside world could appreciate. "I could have done just some random back-packing that would have been just as good for me," says Booth, "but it wouldn't have looked like an achievement on my résumé. I know that sounds insane." Instead, Booth put "1991, Backpacked across America on the Pacific Crest Trail" at the top of his résumé. He even included a newspaper article written about him while on the trail. "In job interviews, I didn't hide it—I boasted about it," says Booth. "I tried to wash away doubts they might have had that it was irresponsible." Interviewers were impressed, and he landed a good job at Boeing just a few months after he started looking.

When Boston architect Ani Baker traveled throughout Asia and Europe for eight months with her husband, she made contact with historic preservationists in each town. Sometimes it was as simple as hooking up with an English-language walking tour. Sometimes she made contact with professional organizations. But she made her presence known. Here's the smart part: her résumé now reads "studied and recorded historic buildings from the 1650s to 1850s in Amsterdam, Saigon, Berlin, and throughout Soviet Georgia." Her husband, Chris, a commodities dealer, made sure their week's stay in Berlin coincided with a free-trade conference—and made international contacts.

The Irresistible Power of Envy

This one takes skill. Once you've arranged your sabbatical, your goal during your time off is to let others in your field know what you're up to without shamelessly plugging yourself. Hone your letter-writing skills. You want people to live vicariously through you—and you want potential employers to know that you're out there acquiring the skills they need and becoming a more fascinating person at the same time. If you come across a sweater factory in Peru that's cut costs by 15 percent through a simple machinery change, drop a line to your coworkers at the sportswear factory back home. If you've graduated from Russian classes in St. Petersburg, send out a batch of postcards to friends, coworkers, and acquaintances announcing (in the native language with translation below) your accomplishment. If you're volunteering as a bookkeeper for a rock band on tour (yes, this can be done!), send E-mail messages from the road as you wind your way around the country. The point is not that you walk out of your adobe hut each morning with your eyes peeled for a job insight. But if you do see something that you think would interest others, then take ten seconds and let them know. It won't hurt you now, and it'll definitely help you later.

If It Works for You, Cultivate
a Larger-Than-Life Image

Ed McCabe is in the image field; he's one of the country's flashiest and most successful advertising executives. So when he took a year off, he conjured up a romantic goal: to enter the Paris-to-Dakar road race, billed as the most dangerous race in the world. He also arranged to write an article for

Esquire about the experience (thereby keeping his name in the minds of potential clients) and later came out with a book.

Admittedly, not everyone is as good as McCabe at self-promotion. And a lot of us wouldn't even want to be. But if you're in a fairly visible position, you may draw publicity to yourself simply by your choice of sabbatical.

At the height of her success at Apple Computer, CFO Debbie Coleman took five months off to start an ambitious five-day-a-week exercise program and to read "several boxfuls of books." In a series of newspaper and magazine articles over the next six months, publications from *Working Woman* to the *Seattle Times* told her story. As Coleman said at the time, "Our problem is with our notion of success, which means 'move up the corporate ladder and stay there even if you're unhappy.' " Coleman may not have planned it that way but her time off (and her provocative insights into it) gave journalists an excuse to write about her—and it helped continue her legend in the high-tech field. Today she's president of the Merix Corporation, a technology firm in Oregon, and is considered one of the most prominent women in her field.

USE YOUR SABBATICAL AS A STEPPING STONE TO ANOTHER JOB

You can get a bit more aggressive about your job pursuit during your time off. Simply arrange to learn from the world's best teachers without paying the price of tuition. If planned just right, a sabbatical can offer you a little-known opportunity to get inside careers and companies you admire and meet the people in them who are the movers and shakers.

Here's how it works: you pick a company or organization that intrigues you, and you offer yourself as a temporary "apprentice" or a "corporate exchange student."

You don't go through the personnel department. You don't say that you want a full-time job there. You don't even exist on the official employee rolls. You merely say you'd like to come work with them for four months or seven months or a year. To up your chances, target a corporation or organization that could really use help because of a sudden growth spurt or painful personnel cuts. It's tougher to break into Microsoft, for example, than one of the foreign offices of IBM or a multimedia start-up firm. Likewise, an agency facing cutbacks like National Public Radio or the Endowment for the Arts would be much more receptive than, say, the Republican National Committee. If you're a lawyer and want to do some good in the world, you volunteer to do legal work for an environmental organization or some other non-profit group. If you're a banker who loves art, you balance the books at a local auction house for five months. The point is twofold: (1) you want to set yourself apart from the unwashed masses of job seekers in your field; and (2) you want a cool, clever way to dip a toe into a new job pool, without taking a complete plunge.

When one of the authors of this book, Hope Dlugozima, took a sabbatical, she carefully nurtured newfound skills that then allowed her to leapfrog to a whole new job. That's because she planned her year off as truly a year *on*.

Hope wanted to move into television, but the media company where she was working was progressing too slowly in that direction to suit her. She wangled a paid one-year sabbatical from her employer by promising that she'd go off on a fact-finding mission and return as a TV expert. Then she offered herself to the Fox Network as an "unpaid apprentice." Her proposition: the people at Fox would teach her TV and, in return, she'd give the network—for free—her blood, her sweat, and the accumulated journalistic contacts and ideas she'd spent ten years developing. The budget-scarred Fox said yes to her proposal, and four weeks later she was a producer on a nationwide talk show. (You might be wondering what happened to Hope's old job. By the time her sabbatical year was through, her company—battered by bad business decisions—laid off 25 percent of the workforce, including her.)

Let's take a closer look at how Hope made this work. She was nervous about what she was trying—after all, isn't it sort of, well, odd to send letters to major corporations offering to work for free? But she also knew that the networks were in bad financial shape. And she knew that creative bosses were looking for creative solutions. Hope tried PBS, *Prime Time Live,* and the *MacNeil-Lehrer Report*—no luck. "I didn't hear back at all from most of the letters I sent," says Hope. "Or I just received confused, wandering phone calls that went nowhere." But at Fox, she found an offbeat boss willing to give her a try. Fifteen months later, when her job search began in earnest, she found out that her résumé building had paid off. "I came back into the job market with (1) high-profile TV experience and (2) an aura of being a risk taker. That alone was enough to get me interviews." Because she now had solid print and television experience, she landed a plum job at a multimedia company in Portland, Oregon.

To try this route, first figure out what you have to offer a company (even a desperate organization doesn't want another person just hanging around the *latte* machine). Think of any specific skills you have that can be easily translated or appreciated in a new setting. Perhaps you're fluent in Spanish and could help expand their business into Mexico City. Or maybe you've mastered a computer technology that could be taught to others. The point is to find your special skill and then offer it. Next, find a contact at the company; this might be as simple as writing clever, well-researched letters to key individuals. State clearly why you've picked this organization or company (you've admired their financial finesse or you're struck by their innovative spirit or other concrete reason). And then take advantage of every opportunity you're given once you've landed the temporary position. Since you're working for free (and, therefore, have a bit more latitude in your demands), you can push to be included in high-level meetings and strategy sessions. See if you can rotate around different divisions as an "observer" or a "consultant." Or ask to be placed on a prominent project. Be as high-profile as possible; this is your chance to bypass the usual entry-level rigmarole. You're an experienced person with a lot to offer. And you're willing to do it for free. Who could resist?

And the end result? You might end up with a job offer from the company. Or you may not. But at the very least you'll have more options, more experience, and more insights into your next move.

Look for Unexpected Career Opportunities

Andy Rohm, an engineer, was working at a computer company in Detroit when he decided to quit and move to Australia. His decision came four days after he'd run the Detroit marathon. "I had been thinking about Australia, but I hadn't done anything," says Rohm. "I wanted a leave of absence, but I hadn't asked. I was in the middle of this horrible meeting. . . . I mean it just went for hours and we weren't saying anything that hadn't been said four dozen times before, and suddenly some magical light went off in my mind and I knew I had to get out of there. I looked at my boss and thought to myself, 'You know, Andy, if you don't do it now, you're never going to do it.' So, afterward, I went into his office and we talked. It was like taking a dive off a 200-foot bridge. I explained why I was going and I didn't have a lot of the answers yet, but I knew I was going."

It wasn't even a Friday.

The next day, Rohm called his travel agent and booked a flight. Two weeks later he was gone.

Rohm went to work on a sheep station in the Outback. But while he was there, he kept up his triathlete training by working out with a group in Queensland and competing in several marathons. "I started to realize that maybe this was something that I was good at," says Rohm, "and maybe I should do it once I returned." Five months later, back in the States, he applied to the Brooks Corporation (a sporting goods company with an emphasis on the serious athlete) and, with no experience in the field, he got a job there because of his unique experience in Australia. A couple of years later, Rohm headed for Reebok, and another promotion.

Before You Leave, Think of Your Return

If you think there's even the slightest chance that you'll want to change jobs or careers at the end of your sabbatical, set aside time both before and during the break to research other options. Enlisting the help of a career counselor, taking a career-planning class at a local community college, or hooking up with the local chapter of a professional organization, is an excellent way to start. All these sources can feed you information about who's hiring and who's not, about how to break into a particular field, about what qualifications are expected from applicants. This is also a great way to make contacts in the companies where you'll want to be an apprentice.

Know the answers to your career questions before the sabbatical begins, so you can lay the groundwork that will help you land a job more quickly afterward. For instance, if you think you might want to relocate to another state at the end of the sabbatical and deal in real estate, you may discover that qualifying for and receiving a real estate license can take several months. If you get your paperwork completed prior to the sabbatical, your application should be through the bureaucratic pipeline and ready to be processed by the time you wrap up your break.

Try Out a New Life

If your new career after the sabbatical might include a geographic move too, see if your time out can include a lengthy look at what you've got planned next.

Coauthor David Sharp, for example, used a three-month sabbatical to travel around the country with his wife, Sheila, and check out other regions. He didn't just vacation in various spots, though. He rented an apartment and took his regular career as a writer and editor along with him. He found out not only about the tourist attractions but what it was like to live and work in each spot. He and Sheila visited grocery stores and neighborhood meetings and doctors and bookstore signings and all the other normal stops of everyday life. Then they were able to decide whether the city felt comfortable to them as a long-term home. Five months after the sabbatical ended, they left their home in the mountains of Tennessee and moved to Portland, Oregon.

USE A SABBATICAL TO REINVENT YOUR OLD JOB

Changing careers isn't your only option. It may be that your job just needs a tweak here and there to make it a good fit for you again. Or maybe you need to pull back on some of your responsibilities and reconnect with the parts you love about your job.

Ted Wright is a counselor at Emerge, a center in Boston that works with abusive men. "My work is highly anxiety provoking," Wright says. "And I've always been very interested in trading money for time and looking for ways to create stretches in my life." That chance came when Wright decided to take eight months off and travel through Europe. Part of his trip was sheer escapism, "wanting to get away from pressure, wanting to be able to sleep." And part was running *toward* something: "I wanted to do some things differently, to get some perspective about my life." He also didn't want to walk away from his work. Before he left Boston, he wrote letters to similar clinics in England and Ireland. When he arrived, he set up group sessions for a set fee. "I was like a cowboy. I'd come into town, argue with men, and then head out. I didn't have to do the follow-up. I didn't have to do the paperwork. I did only the parts of the job I enjoyed."

If you already feel passionate about your work, a sabbatical can help you learn to do your job even better and enjoy it even more. Consider the case of Nick Imparato, a professor of management and marketing at the University of San Francisco. When he took two years off to become the chief operating officer—the second-highest position—at a company with holdings in a wide range of businesses, he found that his teaching improved because, well, he'd stopped being a teacher for a while. In a published poll of students (before the sabbatical), he was number four at the university out of several hundred faculty. When he returned, he won the university award for distinguished teaching several years later. "But how I taught before the sabbatical and how I taught afterward were very different," says Imparato. "Afterward, I was more aware of how naive students were in terms of what would be expected of them once they got a job. Second, I became a lot more specific and could give many more concrete business examples. Now students remark that the classes are filled with realistic examples of business."

The sabbatical not only enriched the knowledge base of the faculty. It enriched the university's coffers as well. As an expression of gratitude to Imparato and to the university, the company that hired him donated funds and office furniture to the university. "I took the sabbatical for professional growth, and for a change of pace, but the bonus was that my dean and I were able to leverage the situation and bring back money to the university, too," he says.

The way to rebond with your old job is to bend and shape it to encompass the interests you gained during the sabbatical. If you learned a new language while you were gone, see if you can move into the international division where you stand a chance of actually using it. If you become a triathlete, start up a new fitness program for employees to join. The point is to convince your employer that the sabbatical wasn't just a personal indulgence but a company asset. "My leave of absence benefited my company, too," says Carla Leise, a financial operations manager for Minnesota-based General Mills. "The first thing that happened when I came back from spending two years in the Peace Corps in Poland was that I was sent to Amsterdam to work for General Mills overseas on a year-long assignment. I don't think I would have been the first person selected for that position if I hadn't been in the Peace Corps. When you go off and do something like join the Peace Corps, you're very much on your own. You have to be self-motivated. You can't be afraid to speak out, so you end up being the kind of person who isn't afraid to ask questions." And that kind of person is respected by companies.

Much like what Dorothy experienced after she returned to Kansas, a time-off may open your eyes to the benefits of the job you have right now. John Eklund, a trade buyer for Harry W. Schwartz Bookshops in Milwaukee for fifteen years, took three months off to move to Montreal and write. He spent his days reading obscure Canadian novelists, drinking coffee, and walking the streets of Montreal. He loved it.

Three months later—happier and more relaxed—he returned to Milwaukee and found that the best part of his sabbatical was yet to come. "Probably the biggest thing I got out of this sabbatical was the feeling that I'm coming back to a job that I chose to come back to," says Eklund. "I had the feeling that I'd done something for so long that I wasn't sure how much I was doing it because I choose to do it, and how much I was doing it because it's habit." Even his writing improved. "I just find myself writing more now [than before the sabbatical]. I'm somehow feeling more motivated."

HOW TO SURVIVE A FORCED SABBATICAL

Nobody likes to be laid off or downsized. Even if it was a crummy job, you'd still like the satisfaction of storming into the office and quitting in a self-rightous huff—or, better yet, casually remarking to your boss that you'll be starting a new job in about two weeks. With the competitor. And a 40 percent raise.

Actually, though, a layoff can be an asset because it forces you to shake up your life, and it often comes in some form of severance that you can then use to finance your time off.

Consider the case of Katherine Martz (a pseudonym). A 37-year-old information-systems manager from Chicago, she was laid off with 334 of her coworkers in the spring of 1992. Martz stayed in bed for four days "drinking pineapple juice from the can, watching *The Montel Williams Show* on cable three times a day, and ignoring the cat." Then she took action. One month after the firing, she left for Brazil with her severance money to help EarthWatch coordinate its eucalyptus plantation project (not as odd as it sounds; by planting these quick-growing trees, Brazilians have alternatives to cutting down ancient forests). "I had two choices: compete with 334 good managers all looking for jobs in Chicago at the same time; or do something eccentric, something to keep me from becoming a corporate drone like most of the people I worked with." She added the four-month-long experience to the top of her résumé:

> October 1991–February 1992   Using CD-ROM technology, helped EarthWatch implement planting and harvesting times for eucalyptus forests in Brazil. My software creation led to the coordination of foresting efforts throughout the country.

Her strategy worked. Martz says many interviewers called her in simply because they wanted to find out how she'd done it. Once she had her foot in the door, she talked herself into several good job offers. "One interviewer at Xerox said he'd had the same fantasy, but had never felt it was the right time," says Martz. "Fun interview. No job offer, though." Four months later that same man wrote to say that he'd requested a personal leave and would be going on his own sabbatical.

Interviews at Microsoft—"the smug ones there plan to take, like, five years off once they make a million"—and a small custom-software company followed. Microsoft passed, but a good job offer came from the other. Then IBM's proposal that she join its office in Beijing turned into Martz's dream job. "I had the technical and business skills they were looking for," says Martz. "But I also came across as a person who understood different cultures and could help solve problems abroad. Even what I wore that day—a business-type suit but with this small Guyanian amber necklace on and a carrying bag I'd brought in Brazil—set me apart. I wanted them to see that I could straddle both worlds—their corporate one and the 'real' one. The funny thing is, the other people going for the job were just as adaptable and probably more experienced. But I won."

Martz took a bad situation, came up with a clever solution, had a great time trying it, and had it pay off. She didn't give up forever the fast track and everything associated with it. Instead, she took the scenic route and then merged back onto the highway farther along. And—if you can stand one more painful analogy—in a snazzier car than the one she left in. Martz ended up with a more satisfying job (and life) than the one she had before. You can do the same thing.

Declare a Panic-Free Zone to Decide Your Next Move

Use the time you're out of work for your sabbatical and you're the boss. You give yourself leverage and power at a time when few others feel quite so confident. Here's a strategy you might try: declare a panic-free zone. If you're laid off (and have a severance package or savings or have pursued some of our scholarship and grant ideas), give yourself, say, three months not to freak out but simply to pursue some ideas that have been knocking around in your head. If you have a family, enlist them in the plan. The ground rules are simple: you don't talk of nine-to-five jobs or classified ads for three full months. Instead, you pursue a fellowship in a new field or volunteer to help a high-profile local arts festival, or use your carpentry skills in Portugal or climb Mt. Kilimanjaro. Essentially, you give yourself permission to look at all your career and life options and to truly use your time off instead of heading right back to the grind. What might be the result of this experiment? You may not get a job as quickly as the person hunting full time (and would it have been a job you truly wanted anyway?). And you may have a little less in the bank (or maybe not). But you'll probably also land a better job after the sabbatical than you would if you'd been looking full time since that first humiliating day of joblessness.

To understand, let's look at it from the perspective of a future boss. An employer—willing to offer big bucks and an office with a view to some lucky applicant—is looking at two résumés. The eager man and bright woman are both of about equal skills and background. On one application, it's obvious that the woman has been out of work for seven months. Her résumé simply lists her latest job, then a time gap. The other hopeful lost his job about the same time. But above his most recent job, his résumé reads:

September 1993–February 1994 Eastern Europe, Asia. Traveled solo throughout the region to educate myself about cultural differences and changing world events. Highlights included a two-month stint as site coordinator, Habitat for Humanity, Soviet Georgia; a 26-day grueling train trip through Ukraine; and a one-week seminar in Budapest, Hungary, on privatization of Eastern European businesses.

Which candidate would you call in? Each lost his job, but one showed initiative. And the same one looks like someone who'd be an interesting interview. Instead of talking with just another person who really needs a job—and all the guilt that accompanies that—you can talk with a risk taker. Hell, this guy may even have some ideas on how you could swing your own sabbatical some day.

Still dubious? Let's see how else taking a sabbatical at the opportune moment might save you. Barry and Leslie Henderson were editors at the *Knoxville Journal* when the 152-year-old newspaper folded. The two, in a trip through Asia the previous year, had visited Beijing and spoken with editors at an English-language paper there. "They offered us temporary jobs but we just laughed. There was no way we could quit our jobs." Then came what Barry calls "a forced sabbatical." The two were told the night before it happened that the paper was going under. "We were to be given six weeks' severance each. The next morning we called Beijing." They spent a year there editing and writing, and then returned to the States—Leslie became a freelance writer and Barry took over the editorship of an aggressive weekly newspaper. But what struck them most is what happened to the other members of the editorial staff laid off that same day. Some of them were in mild shock and sat around for a month or so. Others began ambitious programs of sending out résumés to every paper in the Southeast. Except for a handful of lucky ones, it took everyone about five months to find another job. And only some of them felt truly happy about it. In contrast, Leslie and Barry say they ended up with better jobs—and feel they had an adventure worthy of their fantasies.

Revel in Your Courage

Every time you take a chance during your sabbatical—from playing your guitar in front of strangers to bribing a security guard in Kiev—you're storing up a reservoir of strength that will make anything in the future seem easier. Before your sabbatical, a particular company may have seemed intimidating for you to approach. Coming off your sabbatical, it'll seem easy.

And when you come back and start your job search, you're not going to take the first thing that comes along just because it offers job security. You're going to say, "Look, I know that I have the capabilities of not settling." It's not like you've departed from what you do or who you are; you've just added to it. So now your confidence is a little higher.

James Nelson, an assistant secretary of state in Mississippi, was an Eisenhower Fellow in 1993. He lived and worked in Budapest, helping the Hungarians set up a system to deal with publicly owned land. When he came home, he wasn't the same old James Nelson. Instead he was the new, braver Nelson—and one ready to search for a new job. "If I hadn't taken this sabbatical, I think I'd be really dreading turning in my resignation," says Nelson. "I'd be afraid that the only world I'd known was now going to be taken away from me. But once I got out there, I realized there's more in the world and now I'm not afraid."

You can feel the same way.

6

Before You Go

Sometimes an opportunity for a sabbatical presents itself and can't wait. Your employer announces impending layoffs and offers a year's severance to volunteers willing to leave by the end of the month. Or your spouse has been asked to take an assignment that will require a four-month stay in Spain, starting in three weeks. In situations like that, your only choice, if you want to go along for the ride, is to get up and go and worry about the details as things unfold.

In most cases, though—particularly if you're leaving the country or considering something as challenging as a cross-country trek—you'll need to plan ahead. Hiking the Pacific Crest Trail, for instance, can take up to eight months of planning and training. A long stay in many parts of the world will require a passport, a visa, and months of searching to find affordable lodgings.

Don't fret. Planning a sabbatical can be amazingly rewarding. In fact, one of the best things about a sabbatical is that it can be experienced three times: in the planning, in the actual experience, and in reliving the memories. Planning can entail months of leafing through pamphlets and catalogs, mapping out a route, making lists of all the things you want to do and accomplish, and talking to interesting people who have done whatever it is you're contemplating. Of course, you'll also need to tie up a lot of loose ends before you go.

ON THE HOME FRONT

Make Housing Arrangements

Unless you're planning to stay put during your sabbatical, you'll need to decide what to do about your living space. Your options, of course, come down to four choices: rent out or sublease your house or apartment. Time your break to coincide with the end of your lease or the sale of your house. Let your place sit empty, or find a house sitter to watch your place while you're away. Or, finally, swap houses with someone else. (See the Resource Guide for information on house swapping and rental organizations.)

Financially, renting out your place usually makes the most sense, particularly if you can get more for rent than what you'll be spending for accommodations during your break. From that one transaction, you'll have made your home pay for itself, or nearly so, instead of bleeding your sabbatical budget dry while the home sits empty. If you do decide to rent out your home, however, be sure to notify your insurance company. Your agent will probably insist that you convert your homeowner's policy into a rental-dwelling policy, and you'll also need a separate policy to cover your personal belongings. The added cost of a rental-dwelling policy (on average, $100 per year extra) is negligible compared to the risk you run in leaving your biggest investment improperly insured.

You should also require your renter to sign a rental agreement drawn up by your attorney, and you should insist on a security deposit equal to *at least* one month's rent. Appoint a trusted friend or relative to collect the rent and decide when a repair person needs to be called. Also, just to be safe, transfer the telephone and utilities to the renter's name, so you won't come home to a $400 water bill.

Of course, jettisoning your place entirely, letting it sit, or swapping houses with someone who lives in, say, an Italian villa overlooking the Mediterranean, can pay other rewards. If you're partly taking a sabbatical to bring a sense of change to your life, for instance, the most decisive way of kicking off that change might be to move out of your old place. If peace of mind is important to you, swapping houses can offer an intangible sense of security. After all, the strangers living in your house for six months are more likely to take care of it if they know that you're living in *their* house. Swapping houses can even be a passport to a whole new lifestyle, complete with car, neighbors, a soul-stirring view, even a membership at the local health club. Decide carefully. After all, your own circumstances will determine which option is best for you.

Find a Safe Place for Your Stuff

By stuff, we mean the flotsam of your life that's not essential enough to take along on the sabbatical but too essential to throw away—your furniture, books, clothes, pets. If you're planning to travel and rent out your place, your stuff will need a home while you're away from home. The easiest thing to do with the heavy items, like pianos and massive couches, is to spare yourself a backache and leave them right where they are. Not only do you save yourself storage costs but you can get away with charging a higher rent to your tenants, because the place comes furnished.

Unless you have a friend willing to let you turn half his basement into a storage facility, you'll probably need to rent a storage garage to store your smaller, personal items. Be forewarned that your possessions don't remain frozen in time when they go into a storage facility. You'll need to take some precautions to keep your belongings safe. Here's how:

• Be aware that not all of your belongings should be placed in a typical metal-roof storage unit, where the temperature and humidity can fluctuate wildly in the course of a year, and where climatic changes can grow fur on your prized Picasso etching. Store smaller valuables—jewelry, important papers—in a safe-deposit box at the bank. Precious heirlooms, art objects, and other delicate items too large to fit inside a safe-deposit box should be placed in specially equipped climate-controlled storage units.

• Choose a storage facility that's well secured, and invest in a good lock. Expect to pay at least $100 for a padlock that not even a locksmith can pick.

• Have a trusted friend check the storage facility at least once a month to make sure rain isn't leaking in and damaging your goods. (To gain access, your friend should be listed on the rental lease as the caretaker of your property.)

• Set your stuff on wooden pallets rather than directly onto the floor. The pallets allow air to circulate underneath your belongings and prevent moisture damage that can arise when possessions are placed directly on a concrete floor.

• To keep dust off your furniture, cover everything with cloth sheets. Never use plastic dropcloths, which hold in moisture that can damage your belongings.

• Thieves will go straight for your most valuable stuff if you store your belongings in cardboard boxes with the contents listed on the outside of each box. Identify each box only by number, and list the contents of each numbered box on a sheet of paper kept somewhere other than at the storage facility. Store electronics, guns, and other easily pawned items out of plain sight. Burglars may decide that your mountain of belongings isn't worth digging through if no valuable items are visible.

• Take a photograph of your fully loaded unit, so later on you can tell at a glance whether your belongings have been messed with.

Deal with Your Wheels

If you don't plan on using your car during your break, you'll want to do something more than leave it out on the street. Your choices, therefore, are to sell it, loan or rent it to someone you trust, or put it in storage. The obvious advantage to selling your car is that you'll raise a tidy sum of cash and save yourself the cost of storage and insurance. The downside is that you'll need to buy another car at the end of your sabbatical, when your finances might be at their lowest. Also, if you sell your car and cancel your auto insurance, insurance companies will automatically view you as a higher insurance risk—and charge you higher rates—when you reapply for auto insurance at the end of the sabbatical. You'll remain in the high-risk pool for six months before being allowed to purchase cheaper, low-risk coverage. (One way around that nuisance is to stay best buddies with your insurance agent. When informed about your sabbatical, the agent may be willing to keep your file on hold and save you from having to lose your low-risk status.)

Loaning or renting your car to someone else carries with it all the benefits and drawbacks of renting your house. You'll have somebody to look after its upkeep and possibly even help with the payments, but probably nobody will be as finicky as you are about keeping it clean. Here again, check with your insurance agent before you loan your car. If you maintain ownership of the car, you'll continue to be responsible for the insurance coverage. Your insurance company will insist, however, on adjusting the premiums to conform with the driving record of the person borrowing your car, so make sure the borrower is a responsible driver. (Your insurance can be canceled outright if the insurance company discovers that your car is regularly being driven by somebody not listed on your policy.) If you want the car to be covered under the borrower's policy, you may have to sign over the title to him or her (check with your insurance agent). Before you do that, have your attorney draw up the necessary papers to ensure that the title will be returned to you at the end of the sabbatical.

If you want to avoid the hassles of loaning your car, simply store it. There's more to storage, however, than simply putting a padlock on the garage door. Cars are meant to be driven regularly, and unless you do certain things to ward off mechanical deterioration during the months you keep it locked away, you'll come home to find a 3,000-pound paperweight sitting in the breezeway. Consult with your mechanic for storage precautions unique to your make and model. In general, you'll be advised to disconnect the battery and store it on a wooden surface, put fresh fluids in the car, wash and wax the exterior, set the car up on jack stands (make sure that the suspension remains in the position it would be in if the car were sitting on the tires, and make sure the tires are off the ground), cover the car with a breathable dropcloth, and keep the vehicle in a garage that's heated in the winter.

Whatever you decide, make sure that you maintain a valid driver's license while you're away. If you let it lapse, you'll be swimming in the high-risk insurance pool for the next three years, when you reapply at the end of your sabbatical.

Take Care of Your Health

A few months before your break begins, treat your body to the same kind of thorough checkup that you'd insist on for your car before a long road trip. See your shrink (if only to convince yourself this *is* a sane thing you're doing), get that cracked tooth capped, get a mammogram and a PAP smear, the works. If that troublesome molar seems a little sensitive now, it'll feel a lot worse if it acts up when you're cruising down the Amazon or bicycling across Russia.

For obvious reasons, you should consider health insurance the price of admission for taking a sabbatical. Something as simple as an appendectomy can destroy your sabbatical budget—not to mention your life savings—if you have to pay the cost out of pocket.

If you already receive health insurance from your employer, hang on to it for dear life, because you won't find a better deal. If you don't work for a company that offers health-insurance benefits, consider scrounging up such a job at least long enough to obtain the insurance coverage. Even if you quit or get fired, you still haven't lost your grip on the company insurance plan. A federal law known by the acronym COBRA gives you the chance to stay in your company's group health insurance plan for eighteen months. The catch is that you'll be paying the full amount of the premium rather than the 15 to 30 percent amount you used to pay.

Planning to travel to distant corners of the world? Make sure your health insurance will reach that far and that you know the extent of your coverage. Some policies become invalid the instant you step outside the continental United

States. Others offer "worldwide" coverage but exempt themselves from medical problems that arise in certain Third World countries, where outbreaks of things like cholera confound all actuarial tables.

If you don't currently have any health insurance, get it. In general, you'll have two choices: long-term or short-term insurance.

Long-term health insurance—basically, health insurance that has no expiration date so long as you keep paying the premiums—comes in a couple of main varieties: fee-for-service and managed care. Though individual policies vary tremendously, both types of long-term insurance typically pick up the tab for a wide gamut of medical treatment, encompassing everything from intensive care to a chest X ray. Both types also typically require you to pay a deductible of a few hundred dollars or more—sometimes vastly more—before the coverage kicks in, and depending on the laws of your state, you may have to pass a health screening in order to qualify for coverage (note that some states offer a "high-risk insurance pool" that provides affordably priced health insurance for residents unable to afford health insurance because of preexisting medical conditions). With fee-for-service insurance, you also have to make co-payments of about 20 percent until the cost of your health care rises above a certain limit (usually $5,000 to $10,000). From then on, the insurance generally pays 100 percent of your medical costs. Consequently, even if you own fee-for-service insurance you also need cash on hand to cover the deductible and co-payments. The advantage of fee-for-service insurance is that it gives you total freedom to choose any doctor or hospital—an important option for anybody planning to travel (although the coverage may not extend to some foreign countries, so check with your insurance agent before you depart).

Managed-care insurance, on the other hand, pays virtually all your health-care costs (aside from a nominal charge per doctor visit) after you exceed the deductible, and the monthly payments are typically lower than what you'd pay for a fee-for-service policy. The catch is that you'll be limited to medical facilities affiliated with a specific health-maintenance organization (a subset of managed care, called preferred-provider insurance, allows you to seek the services of any physician, but you'll pay less if you use physicians affiliated with the HMO). A managed-care policy may make sense if you intend to spend your sabbatical within a short drive of a medical facility that participates in your plan. Managed-care policies generally waive the affiliated facility–only rule if you need on-the-spot emergency treatment. The downside to long-term insurance of either type is cost, which ranges from reasonable to outrageous depending on the laws of your state, the condition of your health, and the policy that you choose.

Short-term health insurance will cover you only for a specific number of months. This approach makes sense if you know, for instance, that you'll be stepping straight from your sabbatical into a job that includes health insurance as part of the compensation package. The advantage of short-term insurance is that you're less likely to be turned down because of a preexisting medication condition. One drawback to the short-term approach, though, is that you'll probably be covered only for hospitalization, not for more minor procedures. Another drawback is that you'll have to pay the full amount of the coverage upfront, rather than in installments. A third drawback is that most short-term policies are nonrenewable, meaning that when the policy expires, you won't be able to sign up again (and good luck trying to find a policy that extends beyond six months). Expect to spend at least $250 for a three-month policy and twice that for six months of coverage.

If you'll be spending part of your time in a destination so remote that the cost of being evacuated would be prohibitively expensive, you might also consider buying emergency medical evacuation insurance. Prices and coverage vary dramatically, so be sure to shop around and read the fine print.

In fact, rather than wrestle with these choices on your own, the complexities of insurance are such that you really should sit down with an independent insurance agent who specializes in health coverage. The agent will match you up with a policy that best meets your needs and finances (make sure your agent is well aware of your sabbatical plans). For further advice about health insurance, call the office of the health commissioner in your state—you'll usually find the number in the blue "Government" pages of the phone book—and ask to speak with a compliance officer who deals with health insurance.

Get Your Finances in Order

Long before you begin your sabbatical, you'll need to sit down with your accountant or financial advisor (see the Resource Guide for a list of helpful leads) and figure out your budget. How much will everything cost? Where might you cut back? Is it better to rent a car in Argentina, or would you be better off buying a used one? Now is the time, too, to begin looking into any grants or scholarships you might be eligible for (application deadlines come up every month) and to set up internships or work programs.

Eventually, you'll also need to choose someone you trust to look after your finances and pay your bills while you're away. Of course, you can make that task much easier by arranging automatic withdrawals from your bank account for as many expenses as possible, by prepaying bills yourself, and by canceling as many expenses as possible. Why pay $50 per month to a health club that you haven't attended since last January? (If you think you might want to rejoin the club after the sabbatical, look into whether your club offers "sabbatical status," which cancels all dues during your absence and allows you to return to the club at some future date without having to pay the initiation fee again.)

No matter how much you trust your designated bill payer, you probably wouldn't want to give the person a stack of blank checks and total access to your life savings. Instead, set up a separate checking account and stuff it with however much money will cover your bills, plus some extra emergency funds in case the plumbing backs up during your absence. Then have your attorney set up what's called a Limited Power of Attorney, which gives your caretaker control only over the pool of money in the checking account. If your property suddenly gets hit with a sewer assessment and you're 6,000 miles away, your stand-in will be able to pay the bill without having to get your signature on the check.

Choose a School for Your Kids

If you have school-age children, one of your most crucial decisions will be what to do about their education. At least six months before you leave, sit down with your child and take a look at your choices. You have at least four good alternatives:

• Send your child to a school in the area where you'll be living. Part of what's so appealing about a sabbatical that takes you far from home is meeting other people and getting immersed in other cultures. Enrolling in a local school lets your son or daughter meet potential playmates, pick up a second language, and become part of a different culture quicker than might happen otherwise. If your child is age 10 or younger, you might try placing him or her in the public school system of the country where you're temporarily residing; younger children tend to have an easier time adjusting to language barriers. An older child might attend an "international" school, common in most of the world's major cities. Classes are generally taught in English, and your child's classmates will be children of diplomats, international business executives, and wealthy local citizens. The downside is that your child may be taught at a considerably faster or slower pace than his classmates back home, resulting in a tougher reentry when you get back.

• Ask your child's current school to set up a long-distance learning program. At least three months before departing, make an appointment with your child's teacher. Make your strongest argument: "I've been offered a fellowship in Kenya, and I don't want Catherine to fall behind her classmates." Then work out the details. Maybe the teacher can provide you with lesson plans, homework assignments, and tests. And you take over the actual teaching responsibilities. (It's a lot easier than you might think when you're teaching only one or two kids.) If you're gone for, say, three months or less, you might take an entire semester's teaching materials with you. If you'll be gone longer, arrange to send and receive tests and lesson plans by mail, computer, or fax.

• Use a correspondence school. Correspondence schools have been around since the late 1800s, and offer a great choice for sabbatical takers who will be traveling a lot. Here's how it works. You give the school an address—or series of addresses—and let it know where you'll be on certain days, and once a month the school will mail you a box filled with everything you'll need: textbooks, notepads, lesson plans, exams, letters from other children in the school, even pens and pencils. Using the Teacher's Guide, you set up your own classroom of sorts. Then you drop the tests back in the mail. The next time you sail into a friendly port—or drive into the next village—there's a box waiting with the graded tests and other suggestions.

• Teach your children yourself, using your own wits and wisdom. Why not? Home schooling is exploding, and for good reason. Daily life is filled with potential lessons in everything from geography to history to science. And what could be better than one-on-one instruction? Still doubtful? Arrange to talk with parents in your area who are teaching their children at home. (You can usually find them through computer bulletin boards or organizations listed in your local paper.) And ask if you and your children can spend a day or two observing them. You'll quickly get the idea of how things work. The bonus: not only will you make sure your child keeps pace with his classmates, you'll likely develop an even closer relationship.

ON THE JOB

As you learned in Chapter 4, the key to negotiating with your boss for the sabbatical is to make the hiatus a win-win situation for you and your employer. What *you* get out of the deal is obvious: time off. But what about your employer and the people you work with—your coworkers, clients, and customers? They need to see benefits from the sabbatical as well, because they're the people who ultimately make it possible for you to leave. During the months leading up to the start of your break, your highest workplace duty is to win their support. Here's how:

Avoid Overburdening Your Colleagues

If you can, find people from outside the organization to shoulder part or all of your workload. In this era of job hopping and temporary services, contract employees exist for every job description imaginable. If you must shift the work to existing staff, make sure your coworkers feel justly compensated for their extra efforts. The compensation can be any number of things—money, advancement, a quid pro quo sabbatical of their own at some later date—but what's important is that your replacements feel motivated to tend your turf as dutifully as they'd look after their own.

Keep Clients Happy

Make sure your customers' and clients' needs will be so well met during your sabbatical that they'll barely know you're gone. The simplest way to pull that off is to synchronize your sabbatical with your clients' slack time of the year, when they're least likely to need you. Another approach is to work ahead of schedule prior to your sabbatical and use your downtime during the sabbatical to let the clients catch up. If your clients don't have an off-season or normally require you to be on permanent stand-by, you'll need to find a replacement. As we stated a moment ago, stand-ins will do a good job only if they feel some stake in the quality of their work, either through extra compensation, extra turf, or extra status. Factor in ample training time prior to your departure, and give your clients and customers plenty of time to adjust to the fact that somebody other than you will be answering the phone.

Keep Everyone Well Informed

Long before you actually leave, you should send your boss a memo, spelling out exactly how your job will get done while you're away. Similarly, you should send your clients or customers a letter informing them of your impending sabbatical and explaining how they'll be taken care of. Follow up with a phone call (and make sure your replacements do likewise). If you normally deal with your clients in person, schedule face-to-face meetings for the specific purpose of introducing your replacements. Begin transferring your duties to your replacements at least one month prior to your actual departure, so that you'll still be on hand to offer guidance, locate lost files, and provide troubleshooting assistance.

Be sure to express your gratitude to everyone who is helping out during your absence. A thank-you goes a long way. A heartfelt note, along with tickets to the ballgame or symphony, goes even further.

DID YOU REMEMBER . . . ? A CHECKLIST

Having a difficult time trying to recall all the big and little things you'll need to do as Sabbatical Day approaches? Here's a helpful checklist:

At least a year before you go . . .
(On the Home Front)

_____ Meet with your accountant or financial advisor; begin creating a savings plan and budget for your sabbatical.

_____ Begin making lists of everything you want to do or accomplish during your sabbatical. Put reminders and inspiring photos on your refrigerator.

_____ Discuss your plans with family and friends. Start chatting up your plans with knowledgeable insiders in order to gather tips and leads.

_____ Get on the mailing lists of organizations connected to your planned destination or activity; scour the materials for ideas and contacts.

_____ Send away for fellowship, grant, and scholarship applications, and keep track of the deadlines.

(On the Job)

_____ Look into your company's policy on sabbaticals and leaves of absence.

_____ Talk with others within your company or industry who have taken time off to plan your negotiating strategy.

_____ Meet with your boss to work out the details of your leave; afterward, send your boss a memo restating the specifics of your agreement.

Six months before you go . . .
(On the Home Front)

_____ Begin making plans for your children's schooling.

_____ Meet with a travel agent and ask to be kept posted regarding any great bargains that come along. If you're planning on doing a lot of flying, check into special round-the-world tickets.

_____ Register for classes or cultural programs you plan to take during your break.

_____ Meet with insurance agents. Arrange to get or retain homeowner's, renter's, mortgage, auto, and health insurance coverage if needed, and make arrangements to maintain life insurance coverage while living outside the country. (See Resource Guide for helpful sources of information.)

_____ Make preliminary arrangements for house swap or rental.

_____ Get or update passports for all family members. Ask for extra passport-size photos to take with you. (They often can be used for transportation tickets, work permits, and other identification cards.)

_____ Start a to-do list. Keep it handy, and add to it or cross off accomplishments weekly.

_____ Pay attention to sales, and buy any special luggage, backpacks, or other equipment you'll need. Verify that luggage meets the size and weight limits for international travel if leaving the country.

_____ Find a friend, neighbor, or relative who will take care of your pet.

_____ Reserve a storage space for personal belongings.

(On the Job)

_____ Begin telling coworkers about your plans, making sure to point out that if your sabbatical is a success, they could be next.

_____ Find and begin training your replacement.

_____ Take care of all paperwork that will affect your plans when you get back. Thinking about taking the test to get your real estate license when you return? Get the paperwork in now.

_____ Start a to-do list. Keep it in a safe place and add to it— or cross off accomplishments—as you go.

Two or three months before you go . . .
(On the Home Front)

_____ Arrange to extend your driver's license and car registration if they would otherwise expire while you're away. Get an international driver's license. (Call your local automobile club for details.)

_____ Make a will or update existing will.

_____ Make arrangements to terminate lease; leave a forwarding address for return of security deposit.

_____ Get a complete physical before your health insurance expires—or before you leave English-speaking doctors behind. Ditto dental work.

_____ Update inoculations for tetanus and get any other shots needed if traveling out of country. The Centers for Disease Control, at 404-332-4559, can give you the complete list.

_____ Buy an extra pair of glasses or contact lenses.

_____ Arrange for electronic transfer payments to cover regular bills, and set up a bill-paying system for other bills.

_____ Arrange to have your mail forwarded. (See Resource Guide for details.)

_____ Arrange for storage of furniture, car, jewelry, and other personal items.

_____ Start a packing list.

_____ Take care of any necessary house maintenance.

_____ Make a list of names, addresses, and phone numbers of family, friends, doctors, lawyer, accountant, minister, broker, and insurance agents.

_____ Give your address and phone number to family and friends or set dates for when you'll get in touch with them.

_____ Arrange to have an absentee ballot forwarded to you.

_____ Make final arrangements to lease house or to swap houses.

_____ Choose a caretaker to take care of mail, bill paying, and, if necessary, watch your home or apartment.

_____ File and pay any federal taxes owed; arrange with accountant for their payment during your absence.

_____ Pay city, county, state, or property taxes and arrange for their payment during your absence.

_____ Make arrangements with bank or other financial institution for direct deposit of salary or investment income.

(On the Job)

_____ Arrange for any necessary temporary help that might be needed while you're away.

_____ Send reassuring letters to all clients, suppliers, coworkers, and customers, telling them about your sabbatical and explaining how they'll be taken care of while you're away. Follow up with a phone call.

_____ If you own a business, arrange to have your liability insurance extended while you're away.

A month before you go...
(On the Home Front)

_____ Notify utility companies that you will be away and ask to have service switched over to new occupant.

_____ Make list of all items going into storage.

_____ Make list of telephone numbers of repair people (plumbers, electricians, carpenters, etc.) for the caretaker in case, God forbid, the water pipes burst while you're away.

_____ Notify auto insurance agent that you'll be away and make any necessary adjustments in coverage.

_____ Purchase personal-articles insurance to cover clothing and other items you'll be taking with you.

_____ Arrange to take a six-month supply of all medications

and contraceptives you'll need; make copies of all prescriptions.

_____ Address cards to family members and close friends
who will celebrate birthdays, anniversaries, and other
important days during your sabbatical.

_____ Consider selling stocks and other risky investments if
you won't be able to keep track of them during your
absence.

_____ Cancel memberships in health clubs and other dues-
paying organizations, or ask be put on "inactive
status."

_____ Make sure all reservations, passports, and visas are in
order.

_____ Test your camera, tape recorder, portable computer, or
any other equipment you're planning to take. Buy film
and batteries; buy plug converters as needed.

_____ Locate all house and appliance guarantees; give them
to caretaker.

(On the Job)

_____ Introduce the person who will be taking your place to
clients, suppliers, subcontractors, or anyone else with
whom you regularly do business.

Up to two weeks before you go . . .
(On the Home Front)

_____ Throw a party for the people you'll be counting on to
pick up the slack while you're away. Grovel as necessary.

_____ Put furniture and other items in storage; take a photograph of your fully loaded unit, so later on you can tell

at a glance whether your belongings have been messed with.

____ Get a haircut.

____ Buy traveler's checks. Convert money to foreign currency.

____ Place all important papers, stocks, and bonds in a safe-deposit box, with attorney, or with caretaker.

____ Drop off pet at sitter's.

____ Pack. Imagine running to train with all that stuff. Repack.

(On the Job)

____ Send a second letter to clients, customers, and other business associates, explaining *exactly* how you've arranged to take care of them: who will be handling their business, whom to call while you're away, when you'll be back.

____ Leave a memo with your boss and key coworkers, outlining the status of all your projects.

____ Arrange for thank-you notes to arrive in your boss's and coworkers' mailboxes the day after you leave.

Details, Details: Three Case Studies

⎧⎧7

Imagine what you could learn by going out to lunch with people who've taken sabbaticals. Suddenly the deep, dark forest of uncertainty that you're about to enter contains a blazed trail. Because they've done what you're about to do, they know the twists and turns that lie ahead. They also know the answer to many questions you've been grappling with—from little imponderables like whether you should take your pets along on the trip to weighty existential concerns, like whether you'll really find your true calling in life by temporarily dropping out of the rat race.

Fortunately, sabbatical mentors exist all around you, and your own aspirations can lead you to their doorstep. No matter whether you want to spend several months writing the Great American Novel or sailing the Caribbean, you can bet that others have already done something similar to what you're about to do. If you're seeking specific tips and strategies—such as the pros and cons of docking your boat in Dominica versus Saint Lucia—you'll find plenty of advice givers at clubs and associations devoted to your particular topic of interest (your reference librarian can point you to the chapters in your area). Don't worry about being turned away. Nearly everybody who takes a sabbatical is so enthusiastic about the experience that your problem won't be getting them to open up about what they learned, but getting them to shut up about it.

If you're wrestling with some of the deeper, more soulsearching questions that arise concerning a sabbatical, you can direct your inquiries to pretty much any articulate person who's taken a lengthy hiatus. Put aside the specifics of what they did and where they did it, and you'll discover that their stories are often filled with insights so universal that they could just as easily be talking about your situation as theirs.

Until you scrounge up sabbatical mentors of your own, we've arranged for you to sit down for coffee, figuratively speaking, with several folks who've completed their sabbaticals, and who have plenty to say about the experience. One is a single woman who overcame her doubts about traveling alone in the wilderness and completed a 1,200-mile solo hike on the Appalachian Trail. Another is an investment-firm executive who stepped back from a fast-track career to travel through Latin America with his fiancée, and ended up with a better, more rewarding occupation than he had before. The third is an Iowa farm couple who uprooted themselves from the ceaseless duties of a family farm and took their kids to Eastern Europe for a learning experience they'll never forget.

The people we've assembled launched into their sabbaticals with no special advantages—no trust funds backing them up, no avuncular CEO holding open the door. At least a couple of them even wondered whether they'd permanently tarnish their résumés by taking time off. And yet they all emerged from their sabbaticals far happier and wiser than they were before taking time off.

How did they do so well? The same way you will: by

learning that within every challenge is an opportunity waiting to be unwrapped.

LISA PRICE—SEIZING THE MOMENT

Three years into her less-than-thrilling job as the assistant manager of a pharmaceutical warehouse, Lisa Price, 32 years old and single, yearned for adventure, but what she had instead was a palpable sense of discontent. "I felt like I was just putting in the time, that this is as good as life was going to be," says Price. "I had a nice job, good friends and neighbors. But something still seemed to be missing from my life. I would think to myself, 'I'm 32 years old. Almost half my life is over, and I'm not doing what I want to do. I don't want to work in a warehouse.'" She pictured herself doing bold things like becoming a writer and taking off on some great trek through the wilderness. Still, she couldn't quite get around the fact that she had to earn a certain amount of money every year to be comfortable, and the security of a steady paycheck took precedence over goals closer to her heart. "For years I said, 'Boy, I'd really like to hike the Appalachian Trail,' but I was like a dreamer who never does anything to make the dreams come true," says Price.

She had fallen into a rut so deep that only something big could jolt her loose.

Then it happened. She went into work one day expecting business as usual and discovered instead that she no longer had a job. The company she worked for had been bought out by another firm, and the new owners were closing the warehouse. Price, a woman who'd never quite found the time to pursue her passions, suddenly had more time than she knew what to do with. The same day she heard the news, Price went home and dialed a phone number that had been stuck on her refrigerator door for a decade. It was a number to call for maps and information about the Appalachian Trail.

In the weeks that followed, she dipped into her severance money to buy backpacking gear. She also moved out of her rented home, stashed her household belongings in a 10-by-10-foot storage facility, and nearly set fire to a picnic table while learning to light her camp stove. Accompanied only by her two shepherd-lab mix pound dogs Kliban and Maude, she arrived at the Appalachian Trail in early June and spent the entire summer following the well-trampled path from Georgia, where it began, to Pennsylvania, where she lived, a distance of 1,200 miles.

That was four years ago. Since then, Lisa Price has achieved her goal of becoming a writer. Her first published piece was a magazine article based on the journal she kept during the hike. The success of that first assignment led to a job as a reporter for a local newspaper, and it also led to freelance work for national publications that hire Price to write about outdoor adventures.

Her goal of hiking the Appalachian Trail also lives on. Each summer she takes several weeks off and returns to the trail, picking up where she left off the year before. By hiking the trail in segments, she should reach its endpoint in Maine within a year. What draws her back to the trail time and time again is not the final destination, however, but the journey itself. "The trail puts me back in the right mode again," says Price. "It's like a refresher course in the things that really matter."

Here, in Price's words, are just a few of the things she's learned:

On Being a Novice

When it came time to do the hike, I almost backed out because I had very little experience in the woods. The only other time I'd ever been camping, I'd slept right next to a car. I'd never worn a backpack until it arrived UPS. And I now was going to walk six miles away from a road, put up my tent in the woods, and then keep going in deeper and deeper and deeper. I was afraid of the dark, thunder, snakes. And I started thinking, Maybe I'm risking a lot. Maybe something really bad could happen. Maybe something bad could happen to the dogs. Then one of my closest friends, Betsy, said something that really made sense. She said, "If you back out now, you're going to be sorry for the rest of your life. This is your chance, so you've got to do it. You can do it." Without her encouragement, I might never have gone forward.

On Cash Flow

I spent about $1,000 to get ready for the hike. I bought good equipment, but I didn't buy top-of-the-line gadgetry. I still have the same pack, the same sleeping bag, the same tent, and I've never missed the gadgets. But you could spend $400 or $500 on a sleeping bag if you want the best sleeping bag that there is. I bought a three-season bag for under $100. My pack was probably $70; you can buy a $400 pack. My tent was about $100 or $200. You can live so cheap out on the trail because all you're buying are some basic groceries— noodles, oatmeal, granola, and crackers.

Right before the hike, I moved out of where I was living and put all my stuff in storage. I prepaid the storage costs so I wouldn't have any bills to worry about during the hike. Betsy picked up my mail while I was away, and if anything looked important, she would open it. I didn't want to carry large sums of cash on the trail, so I divided up my money and had Betsy send it to me in traveler's checks. In case somebody ever tried to rob me, I kept $5 or $6 in my backpack so I could say, "Here's all the money I have." Then I stashed the other money in the dog pack, because I figured nobody's going to rob a dog.

On Being a Woman Traveling Alone

The first couple of nights on the trail, I was so scared, I think I fell asleep out of sheer exhaustion. My dogs were house dogs, and they'd bark at nothing. They were probably just as scared. It's illegal to carry firearms on the trail, but I had a pocketknife, and I slept with the blade open the first couple nights out, so I'd have something to defend myself with. But I got to where I realized no animal was going to hurt me, and no person was probably going to hurt me, either. How many muggers are going to hike up in the woods to do their crime? You're probably more in danger in your daily life than you are in the woods.

Men are actually very respectful to women out on the trail. They don't treat you like, "Oh, baby!" It's more like, "How are you doing, where are you from?" Maybe it's the shared experience, the shared hardships, or that they know you're out there because you like the outdoors. You're not going to be out there just to meet them. If you go to a bar and get all dressed up, I think somewhere in the back of their minds they think you are doing that for them and them only. But in the woods there's no pretense—no makeup, no flash. You just are who you are.

The trail guidebooks warn you not to camp in view of a road, not to tell people in towns what your plans are, and not to tell people that you're traveling alone. But it seemed like everybody I met during the hike would ask right away, "Are you all by yourself?" They probably didn't mean anything by it. In fact, sometimes I'd stop at a local post office, and there'd be these surprise boxes sent ahead by people I'd just met for fifteen minutes at a park or along the road. One couple sent me two new pairs of socks. Somebody from North Carolina sent me grits. You just have to trust people sometimes, but there were some people that I just out and out lied to, because something just didn't seem right about them. You just start to get this sense about whom to trust and whom not to trust.

On Traveling Light

I started with a pretty heavy pack and quickly learned that the things I didn't use every day weren't necessities. The first time I stopped at a post office, I sent six pounds of stuff home. Then a week later, I sent four more pounds until gradually my pack went from 60 pounds to 40 pounds. My biggest mistake was packing lots of clothes I didn't need. I should have taken one pair of clothes to hike in, and one pair to sleep in—and that's it. But I started out with outfits— different clothes for three or four days in a row, and it was way too much to carry. As soon as you start hiking, you're sweaty in about an hour, so it literally makes no difference if you wear the same clothes over and over again. I wore nylon running shorts and a tank top, and I'd rinse them out every night and put them on again the next morning. The smell got pretty bad sometimes. Once in a while I'd meet somebody nice, like an old lady out looking for birds, and she'd come up to me to say hello ... and then start backing away. I figured, Hey, if she wanted nature, here it is. When things tore, I just fixed what I had. When I got to town, I'd buy something new if I needed it. In order to fix things, the two items that I found really useful were dental floss and duct tape. Dental floss makes excellent thread for sewing torn clothes. And duct tape will hold together just about any- thing. If you tear your tent or your pack, you can patch it with the duct tape. When my leather boots fell apart, I'd tape them together in the morning with duct tape and cut them off again at night. The tape held them together for ten days until I got to a town where I could buy boots. Instead of carrying a whole roll, I'd just wrap some tape around my water bottle and tear it off as I needed it.

On Traveling with Pets

There are lots of hassles to hiking with dogs, and it would have been a lot easier to do the trail without them. I'd have to stop at a grocery store every five days to buy dog food. Sometimes the trail goes right through the main street of a town in the South, and other hikers would stay at inns and hostels and have a really great time. But dogs aren't allowed in any of those places, so I didn't have the option of staying there. I'd end up hiking a mile or two out of town and camping in the woods.

People would say, "Oh, taking your dogs will be great protection," but that never crossed my mind. I took my two dogs because I couldn't stand to be apart from them for so long, and I couldn't stand the idea of putting them in a kennel for three months. They're like my little family. Besides, I think they had the time of their lives out on the trail. They say that dogs can't really appreciate a view, that they only see one-dimensionally, but they would sit down with me on mountaintops and gaze out for an hour, like they really enjoyed it.

On the Appalachian Trail Diet Plan

I averaged about fifteen miles a day. It was hard work at first, but it became easier as I got stronger and shed weight off my pack and my body. I lost a lot of weight on the trail. I'm 5' 10", and when I started I weighed 140 pounds and when I ended, I weighed 118. I looked like the girl in the ad, YOU CAN TURN THE PAGE OR YOU CAN HELP THIS CHILD. I had enormous knees all of a sudden. My legs were like tree trunks. My ribs were really prominent. I'd always wanted cheekbones, and they showed up on the trail.

Some hikers pack up all their groceries and mail them on ahead. If you can buy things in bulk at home and divide it up, it's cheaper than buying things along the way. But I found it easier just to stop at grocery stores. I'd buy macaroni and cheese dinners and other inexpensive stuff. I carried a strange little stove called a Zip stove, which burns wood, so you don't have to carry any fuel. Other hikers would make fun of it when I'd bring it out, but then they'd see that it worked really fast, and I didn't have to carry any fuel, and if I wanted to make an extra cup of coffee, I didn't have to worry that I was going to run out of fuel. It's about as big around as a cereal bowl, and it packs up real small. You load in little tiny twigs. A lot of campsites have been stripped of firewood, but you could always find these little tiny twigs. The stove's only drawback is it turns your pots black.

On Staying in Touch with Loved Ones

The little towns located along the trail are used to hikers, and the postmasters know to set your mail aside until you show up to claim it. The mail has to have the hiker's name on it, and the words "General Delivery, Hold for Hiker." I used trail guidebooks to plan out these mail drops ahead of time, so my friends and family would know where to write. I picked post offices spaced about two weeks apart, and there was never a time that my mail failed to arrive.

A lot of times I wouldn't even have to go to the grocery store because my friends and family would send me so much stuff. The first package my mother sent me was so great! It had a 12-ounce container of Arid Extra-Dry Deodorant. Like, what am I supposed to do with this? She'd also enclosed a big thing of Pert shampoo, eyebrow tweezers, razors. I was giving stuff away in the post office. I didn't want to hurt her feelings, so I wrote her and said, "Thanks for all the nice stuff." Then the second town I went into I got all the same stuff. I thought, I've got to put an end to this! So I wrote her and said, "Mom, look, I'm not putting antiperspirant on in the morning. The eyebrow tweezers . . . I'm not going to sit in my tent at night and use them.

On the Agony of the Feet

I thought I had my leather boots broken in well before the hike, but they weren't broken in well enough, and I ended up loosing toenails and getting blisters so bad that I couldn't even tie my boots shut. I even took a picture of my feet at one point because I thought, "Nobody's going to believe how bad they look." I made the problem worse by wearing just one pair of socks instead of two. From the start, I should have worn a thin pair of liner socks to wick moisture away from my feet, and an outer pair for cushioning. Sometimes I'd even hike in cheapo foam-rubber flip-flops I'd brought along just so I wouldn't have to put the boots back on.

Almost halfway into the hike, my leather boots fell apart, and I finally bought what I should have worn from the beginning—lightweight, canvas-style boots. They were much more comfortable. They felt broken in the second I put them on. Each step was lighter, and I actually felt like I was skipping that first day I wore them. I still have my leather boots, and I'm determined one day when I get to the top of a mountain to throw them off.

On Lessons Taught by the Trail

I thought that at some point along the hike I'd have this mountaintop revelation, and it would tell me what I wanted to do with my life. It didn't really happen that way. It happened slowly, over the three-month period, without my really realizing it. I became more confident in myself and realized that I really could survive with only those things that I could carry on my back. Friends tell me that certain facets of my personality became more definite and strong because I had hiked the trail. Beforehand, people could walk all over me and push me around very easily. I would bend a lot and be very, very tolerant even of bad treatment because I just didn't want to make waves. Even at work, I was like, "Extra work? Okay, yeah, pile it on me, I'll do it." Now I stand up for myself a lot more. This is a good trait to have as a reporter. I don't back down if someone gets smart with me or if someone tries to evade a question. I'm more persistent and to the point.

I was brought up in mid- to upper-class suburbia, where every family has two cars and you're always wearing new clothes. I always had new school clothes and never wanted for anything. My travels showed me that I could live on less and actually be happier. The more you work in order to make money, sometimes the less time you have to do the things that matter. I always thought I needed to make at least $30,000 a year to be comfortable. Now I'm making $12,000 a year as a writer, and I'm having the time of my life. I'm not sweating the bills at all. I have time now to raise a big garden, live in the country, go hiking with the dogs, have adventures, and do what I want to do.

JOHN SLOCUM—GOING FOR THE GOALS

At the age of 29, mutual-fund executive John Slocum made the biggest—and what some in his family viewed as the looniest—career decision of his life. This self-described corporate "golden boy" was working as an assistant vice-president at a Philadelphia investment firm, and he was also temptingly close to leaping to another company where the salary and equity package could make him a millionaire within five years.

His future looked bullish except for one thing: Slocum wanted more out of life than a fancy office and high-altitude bank balance. "I wasn't motivated by BMWs and big houses and money, money, money," he says. "I was much more motivated by a good quality of life and by the opportunity to meet new and interesting people."

Acting on those priorities, Slocum wanted to take six weeks off to travel abroad with his fiancée before beginning the new job. In fact, he insisted on it. The future employer balked, and Slocum wouldn't back down, choosing to give up the job rather than give up the break. Unhappy at his present company, Slocum pulled the plug on that job as well and earmarked the severance package he had coming—five months of pay—to tide him over during the trip. Only now, he had enough time and money to take several months off, not just several weeks. And that's what he decided to do. "It was something I really wanted to do, but my single biggest obstacle was guilt," says Slocum. "I felt like, 'What am I doing? Am I really burning bridges that I can't get back over?' Sometimes you just have to take a risk. You know, life is nothing but a bunch of doors, and if you sit there and stare at them, life kind of passes you by. You might as well walk through a couple of those doors."

Others in his family reacted as if he'd walked into a wall. "My dad runs an investment firm, my brother is a hot-shot banker, and they both thought I was nuts to even consider such a trip," says Slocum. "But they're different from me. I was much more influenced by my fiancée, who's Swedish. In Sweden, people work for a while, and then they'll travel. Their lifestyle is so different from ours. Here, we tend to live to work. There, they work to live."

Slocum and his fiancée both wanted to learn Spanish, so they focused their travels on Latin America. From September to January, they journeyed to such countries as Ecuador, Costa Rica, Venezuela, and Brazil. The centerpiece of their trip, however, was the two months spent in Guatemala, where the couple rented a room in the home of a local family, studied Spanish five hours a day at a nearby language school, and soaked up Guatemalan culture.

It was such a rich educational experience that Slocum was inspired to help others learn Spanish just as he had—by becoming immersed not just in the language but in the lifestyle of another country. The result, two years later, is a company Slocum started called AmeriSpan Unlimited (see the Resource Guide), a firm that matches up people wishing to learn Spanish with Latin American families willing to open up their homes to foreigners. In its first year of operation, AmeriSpan had 70 clients. In its second year, the number rose to 700, and the company rang up $750,000 in annual sales—roughly ten times what Slocum had previously earned in the mutual-fund business. Granted, he's currently pouring the profits back into marketing the business, so he's not exactly rich—at least not yet. But at the rate the company is going, Slocum thinks he'll soon earn more money

than he ever did as an investment manager. He also antici-
pates being able to satisfy his travel bug far better than he
ever could in his former profession. For one thing, he travels
to Latin America in search of just the right households where
his clients can stay.

The rapid growth of Slocum's venture is something of an
irony, given that he didn't actually set out to start a booming
business; he only wanted to take time off. But such is the
power of a sabbatical that it can merge two goals that all too
often elude each other: earning a good living and living a
good life.

On Cracking the Language Barrier

When I first set out to learn Spanish, I contacted a couple of
language schools in Latin America, but nobody ever responded. The travel books said to just show up and find
language classes, which made me a little nervous, but that's
what we did. We just showed up in Guatemala, and took a
bus to Antigua, where there are about forty language
schools. We got off the bus, and some little guy who spoke
broken English said, "Spanish school? Spanish school?" He
took us around to a couple of schools, and we picked one.

We spent seven or eight weeks in classes in Guatemala,
where you live with a local family and go to classes five hours
a day, getting one-on-one instruction. With my little bit of
high school Spanish, I was soon speaking and communicat-
ing pretty well. My fiancée got hideously fluent. I was so
happy the night that I told my first dirty joke in Spanish at a
bachelor party and everybody laughed. I don't know if they
were laughing at the type of Spanish I used—I was translat-
ing the joke word for word, which you aren't supposed to
do—but everybody laughed. I remember thinking, This is

great! After four months, I could put "Learned a Language" on my résumé.

If I had it to do over, I might not live the whole time in Guatemala with my fiancée. I might spend about half the time living in a house down the street, because when we were together we spoke a lot of English, when we were supposed to be learning Spanish.

On Money Matters

In Guatemala, our average daily expenses were just about nothing. We paid $95 a week for both of us, and that included meals and living with the family, and we'd take the bus everywhere for 10 or 20 cents. It was very difficult to spend money there.

Nonetheless, cash is still a good thing to have when you're traveling in Latin America, because no matter what country you're in, you can always pay in U.S. currency. I've taken cabs in little remote places in South America, and even they accepted U.S. currency. Also, health care is pretty inexpensive in Latin America, but you do have to pay for it in hard cash most of the time. Doctors won't simply take a Blue Cross card or Visa card. In case of emergency, I kept cash all over the place, in different pockets and backpack pouches. I was finding it for a month after I got back—a $10 bill here, a $20 bill there.

On a previous trip to Portugal, a money machine ate my credit card, and I couldn't get it back for several days. Ever since, I've always traveled with two cards and I never keep them together. Usually one is on my person, and one is in my luggage. Most Latin American countries are now installing money machines that work just like those in the United States, so you can get cash with your card. My Visa card was like the Holy Grail while I was traveling, because I took cash advances on it everywhere I went. I had a friend go through my mail at home and make sure all the bills were paid. I had prepared a bunch of checks for my credit-card and utility bills; I'd filled out everything on the check except the amount, and my friend filled in the amounts as we got the bills. It wasn't a big problem.

It's always helpful to be able to call the United States, and in almost every country in Latin America you can dial a couple of digits, get a U.S. operator, and then charge the phone call to your telephone calling card. In order to facilitate payments, I had my account set up with MCI so they would just debit my credit card every month, so I didn't have to write a check.

On Clashing Cultures

The best way to understand people of another culture is to actually live with them. What I found in Latin America is that the people have a whole different way of interacting with each other. They have much stronger family values, for one thing. In the house I stayed in, they had this wedding attended by 500 people, and they literally were chopping up vegetables for two weeks to make a three-bean salad. We ended up chopping beans with the Little Grandma; that's what we called her, Little Grandma.

It took us a while to figure out who was in the family because there were gobs of people going in and out of the house all the time to watch TV. A TV set was a rarity, so most of the relatives would come over. They don't have any phones down there, so people stop over every day to chit-chat. There was a grandmother who was about 85. A mother that was about 50, two older children, about 24 and 26, and the father.

Everybody ate at different times. The father would come over to eat, and the mother would grab a little bite to eat. The students would eat together. Everybody kind of came and went. It took us two or three weeks to figure out that one guy who was always over there eating was really the boyfriend of the daughter. Until then, we thought he was another son. We were there for four weeks before we figured out that the father didn't live there. The mother told us that she had thrown him out of the house seven years before because he had a drinking problem, but every single night he still came home for dinner. We were there for so long that we saw bachelor parties, bachelorette parties, weddings. We really got to know the family. They were very friendly and went out of their way to make us happy.

On Packing

Definitely take a giant towel. You can use it for everything from a pillow to a blanket to another layer of clothing. You should also take a list of important phone numbers (including that of your bank and credit-card companies), copies of your passport and airline ticket (so you'll have all the information necessary to replace the originals quickly if they get lost), and a list of your prescription medicines. If you wear glasses or contact lenses, bring their prescriptions, too. I wear contact lenses and found that it was difficult to find saline solution in many places, so bring some extra solution along. To deter pickpockets, bring a money belt or a money pouch that you can wear around your neck. Be sure to bring plastic bags of various sizes. You can use them to hold dirty and wet clothes, shampoo bottles that might leak, cosmetics, whatever. In Latin America, you can't always find plastic bags as easily as you do here. I also brought along multivitamins on the assumption that my diet would sometimes be lacking in nutrients I normally get. Definitely pack some diarrhea medicine, antacids, and aspirin. And a roll of toilet paper is nice, because restrooms aren't always fully stocked.

On Getting Around

Most trains in Latin America are slow, and depending on where you are, they're also known for being good places to get robbed. Buses are a great way to get around. In Argentina and Mexico, for example, they even serve wine and show movies on the overnight buses. We usually kept our backpacks with us on the bus seat, as uncomfortable as it was. You've got to be careful about keeping your pack in the overhead rack, because we heard lots of stories about backpacks walking off. When we did keep ours on the rack, we would unsnap the backstraps and clip them through the bars, so the backpack would get caught if somebody tried to steal it. Most backpacks have two zippers on each pouch, and after we had a camera stolen from one of the pouches, I went to the store and bought little locks that held the handles of the zippers together. It's not foolproof, but it is a deterrent.

On Adapting to Third-World Conditions

The first day we were there, my fiancée and I walked into this tiny Guatemalan house with green walls. It was kind of a working-class area, but at the time I thought it was slummy. The woman of the house showed us the bathroom. There was no seat on the toilet. Our little room had a window that looked out onto the family's little porch, which was also their kitchen. It was kind of half outdoors, so you always heard people banging around. There was a big flystrip and a bare bulb hanging from the ceiling.

I was ready to move that day. I told my fiancée, "There is no way that I am going to stay here." She didn't like it any better, but she talked me into staying for a couple of days. We got to know the family a little better, our Spanish got a little better, and we felt a little more comfortable. There was another student in the house who told us, "Oh, we have the best family! With my other family I had to kill twenty-five or thirty cockroaches a night!" The toilet seat thing was a drag, but after a while you realized that they cleaned the bathroom twice a day, and you just kind of got used to it.

On Lessons Learned in Hindsight

I wouldn't have bought my airline tickets ahead of time for the whole trip. I would have left it more open. We found places we liked and would have liked to stay a few more days, and we heard about other places, like Chile, that we would have liked to visit, but we ran out of time and had to catch a flight. It's better to not have such a preplanned schedule. I also would never have flown into Rio, the worst city in the world. It's so dangerous and the water is brown and there are robberies all over.

When we came back to the United States, we blew cash just because we had some left. We bought stuff for the apartment, crazy stuff. We started spending money on the company right away, thinking this was going to happen and that was going to happen. We went through our money faster than I thought we would. If I had it to do over, I would have conserved our cash a little more.

On Blazing a New Career Path

I had originally assumed that when the trip ended, I'd probably move to New York and specialize in Latin American
stocks. A couple of times in Guatemala, I even thought about
interviewing for jobs in Central America. But by month 3, I
felt like, "This is so great! Why don't we do this longer? We
could get a job, and if we only made $400 a month, we could
live very well." I started thinking about how much I wanted
to live abroad.

The last three weeks, we ended up at some beach in Brazil.
We had thought about opening a school in Guatemala because nobody knew how to market a language school from
the United States or Europe. Every day at the beach I had my
pad of paper out. We were going to draw up a business plan
on the beach, figuring out how we were going to buy into and
run a language school. That's how we thought up Ameri-
Span.

The first year after we got back was probably the hardest
twelve months I ever spent. It was worse than when I graduated from college and didn't have a dime. To get this business
off the ground, we were working sixteen-hour days, seven
days a week. What kept us going was that we could see the
light at the end of the tunnel in terms of being able to travel
and see much more of the world. Right now we're traveling
less than a month a year, but ideally we'd like to travel two or
three months per year.

My parents are happy now. My mom always had confidence in me. But it was tough. Last September expenses were
more than I had planned for, and my father came through
with some money, and so did my friends. I put together a big
business plan, a prospectus, and raised about $25,000,
which in the old days wouldn't have been tough to raise on

credit cards. But I didn't have a dime because I'd spent it all on traveling. My dad thought I shouldn't start the company when I got back; he wanted me to find a job. When I told him the concept for the company, he just didn't understand it. Not many friends or family really do. They still don't understand it.

On Returning to His Old Life

There's no way today that I could go back into investments. I don't have the drive for it. The motivating factor, the carrot that always kept me going, was my excitement for investments. But traveling and meeting new people and seeing different cultures excite me more. It's basically been a lifestyle change. My fiancée and I wanted jobs that would allow us to travel, and we wanted jobs that were portable so we could move if we wanted to. I just want to experience life. I don't want to be 50 and realize that I missed a big chunk of my life.

DONNA AND DAVID ANDREWS— STRETCHING THE HORIZONS

You think your life is hard to take a break from? Try being Donna and David Andrews, an Iowa couple with an 800-acre, fourth-generation farm to run, two school-age daughters to raise, no real travel budget to speak of—and a burning urge to see other parts of the world. Though hemmed in by their daily responsibilities, David and Donna, both in their early forties, didn't want their daughters—Katie, 12, and Emily, 9—to grow up without having had the chance to live abroad. And they themselves didn't want to grow old without having scratched their itch to venture beyond the Midwest's flat horizons. "As far back as our first date, we'd talked about wanting to travel, and we've talked about it ever since," says Donna.

The family found their ticket out of Iowa in an advertisement placed in a farming magazine. The Eisenhower Exchange Fellowship program was seeking candidates interested in traveling abroad and sharing their technical know-how with people in emerging democracies. David was intrigued by the opportunity, but he felt that his chances of receiving a fellowship were so remote that he held off applying. It wasn't until a week before the deadline that Donna finally succeeded in prodding him into action.

It was a good thing she did. The exchange program read over his application, interviewed David in person, and informed him a few months later that he would be sent on a three-month fellowship in Hungary. Best of all, his wife and daughters would be allowed to go with him. The Andrewses arrived in Budapest in January, and the family immediately turned Eastern Europe into their cultural backyard. They took in the opera, journeyed to Auschwitz, skiied down Austrian slopes, and struck up friendships wherever they went. Family travel was only part of what the sabbatical was about. Through the clout of his Eisenhower fellowship, David was able to arrange meetings with Hungarian farmers, professors, business leaders, and government ministers, and out of those lively discussions came the idea to create a model farm where Hungarian farmers could learn new food-production techniques.

Whatever became of those original impediments to taking time off—money, school, and work? The fellowship swept them all aside. The exchange program provided the family with a monthly stipend to cover their living expenses and even arranged for the Andrewses to stay in a charming apartment in the heart of Budapest, two blocks from the Danube. The girls attended a public school in Budapest, which turned out to be an even better educational experience than they would have received back home. And the farm—seemingly the biggest obstacle—was really no obstacle at all, because the family timed their absence from Iowa to coincide with winter, when the fields would normally lie dormant anyway.

It's now been two years since their sabbatical, and the family still lives life on a global scale, thanks to friendships made through the fellowship. Since returning to the United States, the daughters have corresponded with Hungarian school chums and have even been invited to spend part of their summer with a Hungarian family. David has traveled to Ukraine for a month to help out on a farm-cooperative project. Both he and Donna are taking Russian-language classes at a local community college, with the idea of beefing up their Slavic vocabulary in case another overseas assignment comes along. And the family regularly entertains an international assortment of houseguests ranging from a Mexican agricultural economist to a Zambian production manager to a Hungarian student.

Such has been the outcome of their sabbatical abroad. The Andrewses might have thought they'd just be seeing another part of the world when they headed off to Hungary. What this fourth-generation farm family actually did was expand their boundaries far beyond the limits of an 800-acre parcel of land.

On Winning Over the Fellowship Selection Committee

DAVID: The program was looking for people who can go overseas, learn something, and bring it back. As a working farmer, I was in a good position to take things I learned in Eastern Europe and apply it here at home. I was also in a good position to speak to the interests of U.S. farmers because I understand their struggles. I'm treasurer of the Iowa Farm Business Association, and I'm on the county soybean association, so I can share what I learn with other farmers here at home. These are all points that I emphasized during the application process.

DONNA: Since 1956, the Eisenhower Exchange Fellowships had a very strict policy that says absolutely, under no conditions, would children be allowed. We really wanted our kids to come with us, and we contacted the fellowship program and persuaded them that our children would actually add to the experience, not take away from it. We argued that their presence would benefit Hungarian kids, because the Hungarians might lose some of their stereotypes of Americans if they could meet our girls. We also said that our kids would open doors for us through the friendships they would make with Hungarian children. We might be invited into a Hungarian home, for instance, because our children went to school with the children who lived there.

David and I also arrived in Hungary three weeks before the kids to show that we were really taking the job seriously, and that the children wouldn't interfere. The kids stayed with their grandparents during those three weeks. When the girls came over, the idea was that if they were any problem at all, we would send them home in a month; if everything was going fine, we would extend their visit for four more weeks. We ended up extending it, and the kids stayed the rest of the time with us, and went home with us.

Right from the start, we knew we'd made the right decision in bringing them to Hungary. The most special moment for me was when we picked them up at the airport and were in a taxi crossing a bridge in Budapest. The bridge was all lit up, and the city was all lit up. The look on their faces—even the older one's, the one who was so upset about having to leave her friends behind—you could just see it on her face. She was almost crying, she was so happy. She was like, "Oh, this is so wonderful!" She knew this was a very special time, and you could just see it in her eyes.

On Leaving No Financial Loose Ends

DAVID: We prepaid our electric bill and our gas bill. The telephone company, believe it or not, told us, "Just wait till you get home to pay us." We also left three signed checks with my parents, and if something came up, all they had to do was fill in the amount and mail it.

I tried to make sure everything was paid off ahead of time, but my bank suggested that I sign a blank "note" [a bank loan for an unspecified amount, basically] in case I'd overlooked any unpaid debts. If any bills came up while I was gone and I needed some money, the bank would fill in the amount of money I needed, stick it in my account, and we'd square it up when I got home. It was a good suggestion, too, because an unexpected bill for $1,200 came in while I was gone, and I didn't have enough money in the bank to cover it. My father told the bank about the situation, the bank put $1,200 in my account, and my father paid the bill.

On Networking

DONNA: Before we went to Hungary, we talked with all kinds of people in Iowa who are either Hungarian or had some kind of connection to Hungary. We did all this research on our own, mainly through a lot of phone calling. They told us what Hungary would be like, what to take in the way of clothing. For instance, they said, "Everybody in Hungary wears boots all the time." And they did! Even though they didn't have a lot of snow, there was a lot of dirt on the streets so that was a real good thing to wear boots all the time. One guy at Iowa State University told us to look up a man who worked at a university in Eastern Hungary. He ended up arranging the best week that we had in Hungary: we went to people's homes for dinner each night, and during the day my husband was invited to lecture at the university. Through that one contact, we saw so many places, so many different farms.

I also wanted to have some kind of work experience in Hungary related to my career interests. My background is in freelance video production, and through my contacts at Iowa State University, where I graduated, I found a Washington, D.C., production company that needed footage of an Agency for International Development project in Hungary. The company hired me to find someone in Hungary to shoot the footage, and I also did archival research to find other footage. From that one project, I made contacts in my field, earned a little money, and did something that I could put on my résumé.

On Schooling

DAVID: We could have enrolled the kids in a correspondence school based in the United States, but if I had it to do over, I'd do the same thing we did: put them in a Hungarian public school. It was really good for them. More important than the education was the interaction between themselves and the Hungarian kids. I remember about three weeks after their arrival, when my older daughter said, "I'm going to the library with Esther." I thought, This is an awful lot like home. Our older girl went to class with students who'd studied enough English that they could talk with her. Our younger girl had only one classmate who spoke English, but our younger daughter also picked up the Hungarian alphabet and language a lot more than the older one, and I think it was probably because she had to. She wanted to converse and play with the kids, and she had to learn some of the language in order to do that.

DONNA: All the classes were in Hungarian, so our girls would sit and do their Iowa homework in the middle of the Hungarian kids' classes. The school was very cooperative. The teachers knew that the kids were mainly there to see what a Hungarian school was like, and the school didn't expect them to know the language or do homework. The kids' teachers in Iowa gave me all of their textbooks and their assignments, and I was their teacher in the afternoon. The Hungarian schools go from 8:30 A.M. until noon or one o'clock. So in the afternoons the kids would come home, and we would work on the Iowa school stuff. When we got back to Iowa, they were actually ahead of their classmates.

On Traveling as a Family

DAVID: When we traveled around Eastern Europe, we traveled by train because it's so inexpensive. One time, we went to Krakow—a twelve-hour trip—and the total cost for all four of us was $123 round-trip. The trains were on time, and they were clean and we adapted to it without any problems. My wife and I carried suitcases with us when we flew over from the States, and the kids brought their belongings in backpacks. We each packed three or four changes of clothes, and that was about the right amount. When we traveled around Eastern Europe by train, we could get four people's clothing in the backpacks, and it made it a lot easier to travel instead of lugging suitcases around.

We were responsible for paying our airfare to and from the United States, but we cut the cost considerably by volunteering to be bumped off a crowded flight. It happened in Amsterdam, as we were heading home. The plane was overbooked, and the airline needed sixteen people to get off. My daughter, believe it or not, had been pestering me to get off in Amsterdam because she'd read about Anne Frank. I told her, "No, I needed to get home because field work was going to get started." When we got to the gate in Amsterdam, the line was almost a block long, and I told my wife, "I don't know how they're going to get all these people on the plane, but if we get a chance to give up our seats, let's do it, and Katie will get a chance to see Amsterdam." And that's what happened. We were bumped, and the airline paid us $400 per ticket, besides free tickets for part of the route for the kids. The airline also put us up in a hotel in Amsterdam. It worked out very well.

On Hometown Reactions

DAVID: Most people in our area thought the trip was a great opportunity for us, and they were really glad we had the chance to go. I did run into a couple of farmers who said, "Why did you have to go over there and help them, when they're going to be our competitors in a few years?" My parents couldn't understand why I wanted to go to Hungary, and I'm not sure they know even now why I wanted to go, really. I also had some relatives who made comments like, "Well, I haven't seen all there is to see here in the United States."

My attitude is, everything you see in the United States to a certain degree is going to be just like everything else, and you've got to get outside the country to appreciate what you have at home. We tried to tell my parents what an opportunity it was for us and the kids. Not everybody has an institution come along and pick up their expenses, arrange their housing, provide an interpreter. I think my mother warmed up to the idea after a while, but my father was concerned that I might be losing income by not being there to run the farm. As it turned out, the farm can sit over the winter pretty much by itself, and I was able to come back and start it up again smoothly.

On Making a Difference

DAVID: I spent three months observing agriculture in Hungary. About a third of that time was spent at the Ministry of Agriculture, another third at the three agriculture universities there, and another third on farms—state, cooperative, and small private farms. I thought when I went, being a farmer and having farmed for twenty years and growing up on a farm, that I would really enjoy meeting the farmers and seeing the farms, which I did. But I found out that I enjoyed even more the meetings at the Ministry of Agriculture. I think a lot of it was that when I was on farms we talked for the most part strictly about day-to-day farming. But at the ministry level, we talked more about farm policy—why they couldn't afford to support their agriculture at the level that the United States could, why decisions were made in the past in the communist system, the reasoning behind it. The conversations were so interesting and intellectual that sometimes I'd come away mentally drained. It's not often that you end a day of work on the farm and can say you feel mentally drained, and it was a good feeling to know that the Hungarians found something worthwhile in what I had to say. There were a number of times when I left a meeting and thought, "Geez, maybe I am doing some good here."

On What They'd Do Differently

DAVID: I'd take some language classes before we went. I met one foreign-exchange family that had studied Russian for six months before going to Eastern Europe, and we should have done that, too. I also wish we'd enrolled in an intensive three-week course at a language school in Hungary as soon as we'd arrived. I was provided with an interpreter, so language really wasn't a problem in any of my business meetings, but in terms of getting around town or getting around the country, it would have been helpful to know more than I did.

DONNA: I would be more brave. When I first got to Hungary, I wasted the first month. Before the girls came and even after that, my husband was busy with his appointments during the daytime, and I kept waiting for him to come home from his meetings. I was waiting for him to come back because I was embarrassed that I didn't know the language, which is really surprising because I was used to traveling on my own and hitchhiking in Europe. He didn't know the language either, but he had an interpreter with him all the time. I did go out some, but it was just for an hour here and then back to the apartment. If I had it to do over, I'd go straight to a community center in Budapest and try to find something to get involved in. I also didn't think that three months was quite enough time. I felt like we needed another couple of months there. Six months would have been ideal.

On Making the Transition from One Culture to Another

DAVID: To help the kids anticipate what they would be experiencing abroad, we brought home a video and some books about Hungary. Writing letters was an important way we stayed in touch with people back home. We all eagerly awaited the arrival of mail. Once we were in Europe, the kids wrote letters to their friends in Iowa, and when we came back, the girls then wrote to their Hungarian friends. It's now been two years, and the older one—the one who was so averse to going to Budapest—is still writing.

DONNA: For having grown up in a rural community, our kids adapted really well to life in Budapest. Within two days, they were riding the subways by themselves, walking over a trolley track, and riding a bus and going to school all by themselves. At first, the older one didn't want to go to Hungary and leave her friends. But when she got over there I never heard any complaints. She got along well with the kids, and she would go with some of her Hungarian friends to their houses after school. They would ask her to go to the library with them after school. She got invited to a birthday party and a dance, things like that. Our younger daughter started speaking a little Hungarian, and she loved it. She did say, "I know Iowa is my real home, but Budapest feels like home. I want to take my Hungarian friends back with me so I can have both Iowa and Hungary."

A couple of nights before we left, my husband again took the children out to the bridge that's all lit up at night, and my younger daughter looked up and said, "Now close your eyes. If you can still see the city with your eyes closed, that means you'll never forget it."

8

Engineering a Smooth Landing

When you go on a typical two-weeks-at-the-beach vacation, the only thing you have left when it's over is a pile of snapshots, a peeling sunburn, and a feeling of rejuvenation that vanishes the instant you return to work.

The events of a sabbatical, by contrast, are too memorable, too resonating, to leave you untouched. Maybe you had the chance to really reconnect with your kids or your spouse. Maybe you tested your physical or intellectual abilities beyond anything you thought possible. Maybe you developed a passion for whales or violin making that could steer you onto a whole new career path. Or maybe you had the chance to remember what it feels like to be utterly relaxed. Whatever the specifics of your sabbatical, they are much too important to leave behind as you move into the next phase of your life.

Okay, we can already hear the objections bubbling up in your head: How can I stay close to my sabbatical pals if we end up on different coasts? How can I keep family ties tight when the demands of work and school throw us back into our old roles of strangers sharing the same roof? How can I go back to crunching numbers when I've spent the last six months reading in the greatest library on earth? How can I ever take an extended trip again when I have a business to run?

Those are some powerful arguments. But aren't they pretty similar to the ones you initially raised when you swore you could never fit a sabbatical into your frenetic, money-starved life? You beat back the obstacles once, and you can do it again. Only this time, you have an advantage that you lacked the first time around: you've emerged from the sabbatical with insights, ideas, and opportunities that can propel you into a far more fulfilling life than you had before the break began.

Achieving a successful reentry is really a two-step process. First, you have to reduce the turbulence that often arises as people make the transition back to work—turbulence that can take the form of anything from postsabbatical blues to culture shock to office politics to a backlog of work. Second, you have to take the best things about your sabbatical and carry them with you into your postsabbatical life.

Here's how to plot out a smooth and happy landing:

FENDING OFF THE POSTSABBATICAL BLUES

Just as you probably go through a range of feelings on the last day of your annual vacation, you can expect a similar emotional roller-coaster ride at the end of your sabbatical. On the plus side, you'll feel elated to meet up with friends and family whom you may not have seen since the break began. You'll also have an overwhelming sense of accomplishment. You'll be bristling to take on the next challenges of life. You'll have a clearer sense of direction, and you'll be hungry to test your new skills and knowledge. Says 42-year-old Barbara Rattenborg, a landscaper who spent two years in Guatemala working as an agricultural extension agent for the Peace Corps, "Once I put on an arm-length glove and cleaned out a cow's uterus, I knew I could do anything."

But mixed in with the self-confidence and anticipation will also be some bittersweet feelings; they typically set in during the final weeks of the sabbatical and may linger for weeks or months longer, before fading away. You'll miss the friends you made along the way; you'll miss the freedom of orchestrating each day according to your latest whim. Exacerbating this sadness is the sheer fatigue and stress that can arise from all the chores you have to do to put your life back in order—unpacking, digging your belongings out of storage, enrolling the kids in school, and going back to work.

That's why one of the most important things you can do at the end of the sabbatical is allow yourself time to regroup. People talk about needing a vacation from their vacation. You also need a sabbatical from your sabbatical. Here's how to arrange it:

Set Aside Transition Time

"A lot of people come home on Sunday night and try to go back to work on Monday morning, not realizing that unpacking, going through their ton of mail, answering telephone messages, and putting things away are already a condensed, busy week right there," says Marcia Lasswell, a Los Angeles–based family therapist and the president of the American Association of Marriage and Family Therapy. "Give yourself at least two or three days to get the mail done, pace yourself with the laundry, and get your time clock back in gear before you go back to work."

The longer you've been gone and the more radical the

cultural shift between your sabbatical life and your post-sabbatical life, the more adjustment time you may need. Lawyer Nancie Thomas required a full two weeks to acclimate herself to life in Washington, D.C., after her six-month stay in the Far East. "I had originally given myself just three days between arriving back in the States and going back to work, and I don't know what I must have been thinking!" says Thomas. "The first time I walked into a Georgetown bar filled with people playing pool and jukeboxes playing loud seventies music, the whole thing just threw me for a loop. Part of it was the sensory overload, and part of it was thinking, 'Oh, my God, I can't believe I'm back here so soon.' It weirded me out. It's really important to give yourself some time off before you go back to work."

When you do return to work, you may initially find yourself puzzling over some of the simplest procedures of the office—how to log onto your computer, how to process a check request. This is to be expected; while you were off having a good time, your brain was cleaning its shelves of work-related clutter. Rather than plunging immediately into your job full force, designate your first week back as orientation week, as if you were hiring in for the first time. In some ways, the job will be new, because both you and the workplace have done a lot of changing since you were last together. Attitude is everything, and you'll be much more successful at adjusting to these changes if you view them as challenges rather than as threats.

Prevent the Backlog Before It Builds

There's no worse way to end a refreshing sabbatical than to be instantly stressed out by the workplace chaos that's developed during your absence. "My desk was piled high with correspondence that was three months old, and there were people lined up for a piece of me," says James Nelson, Mississippi's assistant secretary of state, recalling the morning he returned to the office after a three-month sabbatical in Budapest. "My assistant had his hands full with his own work, so he just kind of did the hot spots of mine, and everything else got passed off until I got back. And the closer it got to my return, the easier it got to say, 'Oh, Jim will be back in thirty days . . . Oh, Jim will be back in fourteen days . . . Oh, Jim will be back in three days.' Things that could have been easily handled at the time were allowed to reach screaming-crisis proportions."

Chaos is a hard thing to clean up but an easy thing to prevent. Never leave your job for an extended period of time without making sure that your work will get done—and that your substitute's work gets done as well. If at all possible, schedule your sabbatical so that it doesn't overlap with the vacations of key staffers. If your staff is already busy, divvying up your work among the remaining members will inevitably create a backlog. Consider using temps, student interns, contract employees, or trainees who'll work as hard as Iditarod sled dogs in exchange for a shot at advancement. If you want your replacements to do their jobs well, you need to give them some stake in the outcome—greater experience, knowledge, earning potential, or turf. Without that incentive, they'll feel dumped on, and dumped-on individuals have the worst attitude in the world when it comes to saving somebody else's butt.

Commemorate the End of Your Sabbatical with a Ceremony or Ritual

Sabbaticals are such enriching experiences that people sometimes resist moving on to the next phase of their lives. Before you can truly look ahead, you need to have a sense of closure. "We have rituals when someone enters a family, when someone leaves a family, and when families are together," says Andres Nazario, Jr., a Florida-based family therapist who spent three months in Uruguay on a Fulbright Scholarship. "Rituals help us mark the transitions in our lives, and they can help us through the transition of a sabbatical, too." There are plenty of ways to celebrate the end of a sabbatical: Invite all your friends over and throw a welcome-back party for yourself. Spend an evening organizing your snapshots. Read your travel journal from cover to cover. Pop open the lager that you brought home from Hamburg. Anything will work, so long as you find it meaningful.

If your kids participated in the sabbatical, be aware that they'll miss all the things about the break that you will—the friendships, the surroundings, the pace of life. They may even identify more closely with the site of their sabbatical than with their hometown. Here's where rituals and ceremonies come in handy once again. "The children need a way of saying goodbye to the sabbatical experience," says Iowa-based marriage and family therapist John Leverington. "It could be something as simple as walking from room to room and having each person recall something that happened there during the sabbatical. You could also have a 'last supper' together, a special dinner for reminiscing about what happened during the last six months as well as what the hope is for what happens next." If you traveled during the sabbatical, you should encourage your kids to find something during the trip that they can take home with them—a treasure or memento from the country or city where they've spent the last several months. This physical symbol of their trip will help them feel that they are carrying the sabbatical experience with them into the next phase of their life. Also, encourage them to exchange letters and pictures and send gifts on birthdays and holidays to the friends they made during the sabbatical. "They'll have a more positive view of the sabbatical experience if the connections they made with others are on-going," says Leverington.

Capitalize on Your Sabbatical

The people who have the easiest time fending off post-sabbatical blues are those who view their sabbatical as a means to a very specific end. If you spent your sabbatical in Paris learning to be a sous chef, reentry isn't so much the conclusion of anything but a graduation to something better. When you plan your sabbatical, therefore, do so with an eye toward how it will contribute to other goals in your life. *St. Petersburg Times* deputy managing editor John Costa, for example, knew long before he ever went on a sabbatical that one day he'd like to be the top editor on a newspaper. He took a year off to participate in a journalism fellowship at the University of Michigan, in part because the intellectual rigor of the sabbatical would be good preparation for his journalistic goal. Soon after the sabbatical ended, he was hired as the executive editor of the *Idaho Statesman*, and he stepped into the post without the slightest need to regain his bearings. The reason: he'd never lost them. "It just seemed that I was taking the next step in the adventure that I'd set out on when I went to Michigan," says Costa. "I felt very secure."

TAKING BACK THE REINS AT WORK

When properly planned, a sabbatical can be your path not just to a fun six months but to a richer, more satisfying work life afterward. But for that to happen, you have to know how to deal effectively with change. After all, in the time that you'll be away from your job, much can happen. Colleagues, clients, projects, and even whole departments can come and go. Getting back into the workforce after you've been gone for several months will seem like the occupational equivalent of hopping onto a spinning merry-go-round: the experience can be rewarding and exciting, but only if you watch your step. Here's how:

Establish Your Niche

As you read in Chapter 4, a key part of negotiating for a sabbatical is making sure you and your boss are in synch about the role you'll have in the company when you return. This agreement should be specific in terms of your job title, duties, and compensation. Most bosses will bristle at signing anything that resembles a legal document guaranteeing these terms in writing. But type up the agreement anyway and send it to your boss in the form of a memo (also keep a copy for yourself). The memo will ward off miscommunication and faulty memories, either of which can put your job security in serious jeopardy.

If you're self-employed, you already know that every business develops a certain momentum that takes months if not years to build up. When first starting out, an entrepreneur practically goes begging for clients, and eventually, when success comes, the biggest concern is figuring out how to handle the demand. You spent too much time building up this momentum to let it grind to a standstill during the sabbatical. The way you maintain it is to contact your major clients prior to the break and arrange to have assignments waiting for you when the sabbatical ends. Lining up projects far into the future accomplishes two things: first, you'll be able to start earning money almost immediately after your sabbatical ends rather than scraping by through the pro-tracted lead time necessary to scrounge up work; and second, you won't have to go to the trouble of calling all your clients at the end of the sabbatical and reminding them that you've rejoined the living. Since they've already slotted you for work, as far as they're concerned you never really left.

Safeguard Your Turf

The hole you create in the company by your absence is liable to be filled by ambitious underlings and colleagues who may not want to relinquish the spot. How do you reestablish your presence? The sabbatical agreement that you negotiated with your boss is your best protection, but timing is also an impor-tant ally. Time your return to coincide with the start of several meaty new projects or with the peak time on the yearly schedule, when coworkers are scrambling so hard to keep up with their own duties that the last thing they'd want to do is shoulder yours as well. Another option: time your return to coincide with the start of vacation (or better still, the start of a sabbatical) for those who took over your duties. Their absence will give you the opportunity to restake your territory without any interference. In addition, take it upon yourself to find and train your replacements, if for no other reason than that you can pick the people least likely to stage a coup. If it's other staffers you fear, delegate your work to contract employees as much as possible.

Share, but Don't Gloat

The danger of being the first person in your organization to take a sabbatical is that you can also become the target of your coworkers' jealousy and resentment. What's more, you'll only make matters worse if you breeze into the office on your first day back and start flashing snapshots of Fiji. Keep in mind that your colleagues are already keenly aware that you were off having the time of your life while they were left behind in the trenches. To remind them of that fact is only to stir up bitterness. So don't you go to them with your sabbatical stories. Let them come to you.

When you do discuss your sabbatical with coworkers and employers, put the emphasis on how they might capitalize on the experience. "Make sure the knowledge that you share with the people at work is something useful, rather than 'You can't imagine how nice it was to sit in John Kenneth Galbraith's class,' " says Bill Kovach, the curator of the Nieman Foundation, a program that brings journalists from around the world to Harvard University for a year-long fellowship. "That's a thing they may never get a chance to do, and you'll only infuriate them when you mention it. What you could say instead is, 'I've been focusing on the international economy, and I've got some ideas about how we can relate the importance of the markets in Tokyo and Berlin to what's happening in our city.' Give really specific, value-added ideas and information, without making it sound like the story of what you did on your summer vacation."

Stay in Touch

During the time that you'll be gone from work, the whole direction of your company can shift in unpredictable ways. If you let yourself fall completely out of the loop during the sabbatical, you'll discover on your first day back that the agreement you forged ten months earlier with your boss— the agreement that specified the title and duties you'd have afterward—now seems as obsolete as the Volstead Act. Your colleagues may snap up all the plum assignments, and you'll be left with nothing but the dregs. Out of sight really is out of mind, and you need to make sure that bosses and colleagues always remember you're part of the team, albeit an absentee member.

No one's suggesting that you spend the entire break with a beeper clipped to your belt. In fact, you want the communication between you and the office to be something that still allows you to push all thoughts of work to the farthest corner of your brain; otherwise, what's the point of taking a sabbatical? One of the easiest and most effective ways to stay in touch is to dash off a monthly postcard to the folks back at the office. Your postcards will likely end up thumbtacked to the bulletin board above the copying machine, and every time your coworkers need to make a photostat, they'll see your message, "Having a fine time in Ghana but can't wait to see the old gang again on June 24th," and be reminded that your absence is temporary, not permanent. Also arrange for someone at work to send you copies of the company newsletter, so you can stay informed about personnel changes and other big events. If, during your sabbatical, you happen to stumble across information that might be useful to your colleagues back home, pass it along. They'll appreciate the fact that you took time away from your break to make their lives a little easier.

During the final two months of your sabbatical, you should increase your contact with the office to a minimum of one phone call every two to three weeks. That way, you can put your dibs on projects scheduled to begin around the time of your return and generally let everybody know that you're about to show up again. During newspaper editor Melanie Sill's year-long fellowship at Harvard, for example, she heard a cautionary tale about a former fellow who literally didn't have a desk when she went back to work, because the rest of the staff had forgotten about her when they rearranged the newsroom. Sill refused to let the same thing happen to her. "I didn't want to unplug completely from work and then resurface a year later and say, 'I'm back,' " she says. "I thought it would be much harder to come back if I did. I probably talked to my bosses once a month, and I subscribed to my newspaper. I didn't read every story every day, but I kept up with the major work being done." Because Sill went out of her way to stay in touch with the newspaper, the newspaper went out of its way for Sill. Far from being forgotten, she received word during the latter part of the sabbatical that she was being promoted from deputy metro editor to projects editor, a position that would let Sill take better advantage of the insights she gained during the fellowship. "Keeping in touch really did make it easier to go back," says Sill.

KEEPING YOUR SABBATICAL ALIVE

Chronologically, all sabbaticals must eventually end. But there's another way to measure the lifespan of a sabbatical—in terms of the joy and fulfillment that it infuses into the rest of your life. On that score, your sabbatical can live for as long as you're able to savor the experience. Here's how to make it linger:

Treasure Your Sabbatical Friendships

These are connections that you don't want to lose, because they usually go beyond the superficial, hi-how-are-you relationships that we strike up with neighbors and coworkers. Like friendships from high school, college, and boot camp, the friendships formed during a sabbatical are often strong because people forge a special bond when they go through a major transition in their lives together.

This bond needn't be broken even when you and your sabbatical friends are thousands of miles apart. These days, anybody with a home computer, modem, and phone line can instantaneously swap electronic correspondence with anybody else around the world, for a nominal price. San Francisco magazine writer Deborah Franklin, for example, spent a year in Boston on a journalism fellowship and became great friends with other journalists from around the world who participated in the program. When the sabbatical ended, Franklin and her pals simply went from meeting over coffee to meeting via their computer screens. "We all obtained E-mail accounts, and literally every day I have on-line conversations or exchange E-mail with at least one fellow," says Franklin. "We talk books. We know each other's professional interests and recommend sources. These are friendships I'll have the rest of my life, and the Internet has been a wonderful way to keep our communications open."

Besides the individuals you know personally, you also share an important bond with everybody else who's ever taken a sabbatical. Essentially you belong to a fraternity of people who understand what it's like to live life on their own terms, to break free of the usual rules of life, and to really give themselves a taste of freedom. Your bond is even stronger with people who've taken a sabbatical similar to yours. You and they will have an instant rapport, because you'll understand each other in ways that not even your life-long friends can fully grasp. Indeed, when you're really aching to talk about your cross-country bike ride, you'll never find better listeners than among members of the local cycling club who've completed the same trek. You'll find these compatriots through local clubs devoted to whatever interest you happen to have, be it camping or genealogy or home schooling.

Your local library probably keeps some record of the groups and clubs in your area. You can also find them through a library reference book called the *Encyclopedia of Associations*, which lists more than 22,000 organizations in the United States. Sometimes it's amazing how specific these clubs can be in their focus. The Central Arkansas Peace Corps Association, for example, is the place where Arkansas schoolteacher Dorothy Gantz goes to find people with whom she can share her memories about serving in Africa for two years with the Peace Corps. "I've also spent a lot of time on the phone with people I served with," says Gantz. "We've written lots of letters, made lots of phone calls, and my first vacation after I'd been home for about a year was to the East Coast to visit my best friend from the Peace Corps."

Save the Memories

There wouldn't be much point in reading a classic like *War and Peace* if you didn't take some time afterward to ponder deeper truths. Your sabbatical is also a great story that deserves to be pondered. During the break itself, however, you're often so caught up in the adventures of the moment that you can't absorb much more than immediate sights and sounds. It's not until afterward that you can really sit back and draw lessons from the experience—lessons that will illuminate your life. For that reason, it's wise to keep some sort of record of your experience—a journal, tape-recorded impressions, a photographic account—to preserve the memories for later, when you have the time and perspective to ruminate about what you've been through. "I kept a microcassette recorder strapped onto the handlebars of my bike so that I would key in on what I was seeing while I was riding," says former paper salesman David Ginsberg, who logged more than 24,000 miles on a round-the-world bicycle trip to raise money for Oxfam. "As I saw something that was worth mentioning, I hit the record button and started talking. It really helped me to live in the present and not start dreaming about things that happened days before or that would happen when I got to where I was going."

Your loved ones will also have a much better appreciation of your saga if they contribute in some small way to helping you preserve the memories. For instance, ask a friend or relative you trust to save all the letters and mementos you send back, so you won't have to lug around a backpack full of souvenirs and diaries. "I wrote a lot of letters and also used a cassette recorder to do oral letters," says Peace Corps volunteer Dorothy Gantz, "and my very best friend saved every one and gave them back to me. I'm so glad she did, because everything that happened to me is in those letters."

Still another way to integrate your loved ones into the adventure is to take along a laptop computer and use it to crank out a newsletter describing your exploits. There's something about the format of a newsletter that forces you to emphasize the dramatic over the mundane. When else will you ever see your life written up in headlines such as, "Joe Saberniak Crosses Equator"? When else will you be able to begin a piece of correspondence with the words, "Dateline: Djakarta"? You can even take letters received from friends and family and run them in the "Letters to the Editor" section of the newsletter. Each installment will make your loved ones feel not just like distant observers of the sabbatical but actual subscribers to it. The newsletter will also tip your readers off to any changes in outlook or lifestyle that you undergo along the way—and they won't be so puzzled by the changes when you return home. Having used the newsletter to vicariously travel along with you, they might have even undergone a bit of a change in outlook themselves.

Reprioritize Your Life

When you take a sabbatical, you often have to live more simply than you did before. You do without the usual amenities in order to save money or lighten your luggage. Where before you felt naked without a closet full of Armanis, you learn to get by on one change of underwear. Where before you always booked a room at a fancy downtown hotel, you learn that the most satisfying night's sleep happens inside a tent pitched deep in the woods. You may also travel to places in the world where people still value such things as spirituality and relationships over more modern comforts like home-entertainment centers and heated three-car garages. Confronted with life at its most basic, you rediscover simple pleasures often lost amid the frenzy and distractions of modern life—the pleasures of family, peace of mind, learning, and leisure.

You can hang on to these simple pleasures after the sabbatical ends, but only if you clear the clutter out of your life and give them the space they need to flourish. John Bloebaum, a map buyer for a large bookstore in Portland, Oregon, spent seven months in the Yucatán, learning about the history and culture of the Mayans. Though he's now back in the Pacific Northwest, he continues to allow his fascination with the Mayans to take precedence over other, shallower pursuits. "I never thought that I'd like to read and do as much research as I now do," says Bloebaum. "Reading was always something that I hated. But now, it's all-consuming. It's what I'd rather do than just about anything. I probably spend ten to fifteen hours a week reading up on the Mayans. It's changed my life considerably. I'm not as much of a consumer as I once was. I don't even watch TV anymore."

Those things that steal time, money, and energy away from your real priorities should be jettisoned from your life. Only you know what's really a necessity and what's not, but you'll never have a clearer idea of the difference than you do right now. Do you really need to reinstall cable if you plan to spend the next two years reading everything written by Dickens? Do you really need to live in the toniest, most expensive part of town when you'd rather use the money to spend part of every year traveling in Latin America? Do you really need to jockey for another promotion when each increase in responsibility makes it harder to pursue the true passions of your life? Rich Birmingham, a Seattle attorney who spent four months bicycling across Russia in 1991, decided that he didn't want to be the office superman anymore if it mean't he couldn't satisfy his urge to travel. "I'd practiced five years as a lawyer and had never taken a vacation because I assumed that the whole world needed me," says Birmingham. "Then in 1983 I spent three weeks in Greece, and it opened my eyes to travel and relaxation. I also realized that life can go on in the law firm without me. So every year since I have taken three to six weeks off on a major trip. Usually I'm in some remote place in the world, and I can't be contacted. When I'm gone, I'm gone. I put a message on my voice mail that says, 'I'm out of the country. If you need help, see these people.' I figure that the work will get done—and it does."

Take Bite-Sized Sabbaticals

Granted, the demands of work will probably stop you from signing up for another California-to-Maine bicycle ride any time soon. But why not pursue on a smaller scale the same activities you did during the sabbatical? That might mean working two extra hours four days a week so you can take the fifth day off for camping, taking a cut in pay to have your afternoons free for home-schooling your kids, or switching from salaried to freelance employment so you can pick and choose your assignments based on whether they conflict with ski season.

Fortunately, the traditional forty-hour work week isn't the institution it once was. Companies are increasingly willing to accommodate flextime requests because bosses realize that anything they can do to reduce the incidence of work-related stress and burnout will help in the expensive fight against absenteeism, lost productivity, and skyrocketing health-care costs. In this era of downsizing, volunteering to job-share, work two-thirds of the time, or work on a project-by-project basis may mesh well with your company's agenda to cut costs and reduce staff size.

Begin Planning Your Next Sabbatical

One hallmark of a successful sabbatical is that it leaves you brimming with ideas for your next big break. Go with that urge. Sort through the shoebox full of travel brochures that you've been collecting since long before your first sabbatical, and come up with destinations that you can begin to research. Make a list of the twenty-five things you absolutely have to do in life before you move on to that great sabbatical in the sky. Then stick the list under a refrigerator-door magnet where you'll be constantly reminded that these adventures are in your future.

One way to make the time pass quickly from one sabbatical to the next is to learn skills that will be useful during your next adventure. If you intend to travel to Central America, sign up for Spanish classes at a nearby college. If another long-distance hike is in your future, join a hiking club to keep your backpacking muscles in shape and meet new trekking buddies. These activities will not only help prepare you for the next adventure on your list but they'll make the time in between adventures crackle with anticipation.

In the same sense that it's better to see the glass as half full rather than half empty, adopt the attitude that your sabbaticals aren't a break from work so much as work is a break between sabbaticals. Get out of the habit of thinking of your sabbatical as a once-in-a-lifetime experience, and view it instead as a once-in-a-while experience. "What I learned from Africa is that you don't live to work, you work to live," says New York City–based magazine editor Sean Plottner, who spent half a year trekking across the continent. "That's been a major philosophical turnaround for me. I can still have a career, and I can still have success. But they are just means to an end. The end is living, climbing mountains, traveling. Ever since I was in high school, I wanted to be a journalist, and the best damn one I could be. Well, I'm really glad to know there's a lot more to life than the nine-to-five grind."

Resource Guide

GRANTS, SCHOLARSHIPS, AND FELLOWSHIPS

ANNUAL REGISTER OF GRANT SUPPORT: A DIRECTORY OF FUND-
ING SOURCES lists nearly 3,000 programs (representing more than
$100 billion in aid) sponsored by government agencies, private
foundations, corporations, unions, church groups, and educational and professional associations. Published by R.R. Bowker,
the $175 book contains such information as the organization
name, address, and telephone number; name of grant program;
purpose; amount of support per award; number of applicants and
recipients for the most recent years; eligibility requirements; application instructions; and deadline. For more information, call
R.R. Bowker, in Providence, NJ, at 908-464-6800. Also available
in most libraries.

NATIONAL SCHOLARSHIP RESEARCH SERVICE publishes several
annual listings of scholarships and also offers custom-tailored
database searches of more than 250,000 available scholarships,
fellowships, and grants. The cost ranges from about $70 to more
than $300, depending on the extent of the search. For more infor-
mation, write NSRS, 2280 Airport Boulevard, Santa Rosa, CA
95403; or call 707-546-6781.

THE FOUNDATION CENTER, with libraries in Atlanta, Honolulu, New York City, San Francisco, and dozens of other cities, has among the most extensive collections of grants resource materials in the country. For more information, call 212-620-4230.

Tips

• When filling out forms for scholarships or other funds, be concise, complete, and—most important— honest. The people who read them want to know the real you, especially the things that make you different from other applicants.

• Try to get your application in a month before the deadline. By doing so you'll give the selection committee more time to read it, and you won't be part of the pack.

HEALTH INSURANCE AND HEALTH CARE

MEDHELP WORLDWIDE offers comprehensive health and travel insurance to travelers who are away from their home country for at least six months. Premiums vary according to destination. For more information, write MW, Wallach and Company Inc., 107 West Federal Street, P. O. Box 480, Middleburg, VA 22117.

NATIONAL INSURANCE CONSUMER HELPLINE, sponsored by the Health Insurance Association of America, offers callers information on travelers' health insurance, including types of insurance available and companies that offer it. For more information, call 800-942-4242.

THE INTERNATIONAL ASSOCIATION FOR MEDICAL ASSISTANCE TO TRAVELERS provides a pocket-sized world directory of English-speaking doctors around the world to its members. Memberships are free, but the IAMAT welcomes donations. For more information, write IAMAT, 417 Center Street, Lewiston, NY 14092; or call 716-754-4883.

THE INTERNATIONAL TRAVELER'S HOTLINE, a service of the federal Centers for Disease Control and Prevention, provides taped information on vaccinations, food and water precautions, and reports of disease outbreaks around the world. For more information, call 404-332-4559.

THE TRAVELERS EMERGENCY NETWORK offers emergency medical care, air evacuation, and prescription delivery anywhere in the world. The annual membership fee is $30 for individuals, $50 for families. For more information, call 800-275-4836.

HOUSE SWAPS AND RENTALS

AT HOME ABROAD is an agent for rentals in Western Europe, the Caribbean, and Mexico. It charges a one-year registration fee of $25, which can be applied to a rental within the year. For more information, write AHA, 405 E. 56th Street, Suite 6H, New York, NY 10022; or call 212-421-9165.

BRITISH TRAVEL ASSOCIATES arranges for mostly inexpensive home rentals in Britain. For more information, write BTA, P.O. Box 299, Elkton, VA 22827; or call 800-327-6097.

HOME EXCHANGE NETWORK offers a computer on-line home-exchange service that promises up-to-the-moment home listings. For more information, write HEN, P.O. Box 915253, Longwood, FL 32791; or call 407-862-7211.

INTERVAC U.S. represents Intervac International, a world-wide network of home-exchange offices, which publishes four catalogs of home listings each year. Members pay a fee to list their homes in the Intervac catalogs. Most of the listed homes are for exchange, but rental listings also are allowed. Participants make contact directly with the homeowners. The cost to place a listing and to receive three catalogs is $78; for seniors over 62, the cost is $73. A fourth catalog is available for an additional price. For more information, write IUS, P.O. Box 590504, San Francisco, CA 94159; or call 415-435-3497 or 800-756-4663.

LOAN-A-HOME, a direct-contact listing service, specializes in long-term rentals and exchanges. A four-month stay is usually required, but that rule is waived during the peak months of July and August and in some other circumstances. The organization publishes two directories and two supplements each year. For more information, write LAH, 2 Park Lane, Apartment 6E, Mount Vernon, NY 10552; or call 914-664-7640.

MI CASA SU CASA provides a forum for lesbian and gay travelers to set up home exchanges and rentals around the world. Members pay an annual fee of $78 to receive two confidential catalogs, published in the spring and the fall. Participants make direct contact. For more information, write MCSC, P.O. Box 10327, Oakland, CA 94610; or call 800-215-2272 or 510-268-8534.

THE FRENCH EXPERIENCE arranges for the rental of simple homes or *gites* in French villages. Accommodations for four can be as low as $300 a week. For more information, write TFE, 370 Lexington Avenue, New York, NY 10017; or call 212-986-6097.

THE INVENTED CITY, an international home-exchange organization, publishes three catalogs a year—in November, February, and June. Members make contact directly. The fee is $50 for a one-year membership. For more information, write TIC, 41 Sutter Street, Suite 1090, San Francisco, CA 94104; E-mail to invented@backdoor.com; or call 415-673-0347 or 800-788-2489.

TRADING HOMES INTERNATIONAL publishes three directories of homes for exchange around the world. Participants make direct contact. An annual subscription, which costs $65, buys a listing in the three directories, including one with photo. For more information, write THI, P.O. Box 787, Hermosa Beach, CA 90254; or call 800-877-8723.

TRADING PLACES, by Bill and Mary Barbour, offers a detailed primer on the intricacies of home exchanging. For more information or to order, call Rutledge Hill Press at 615-244-2700.

VACATION EXCHANGE CLUB publishes three directories of homes for exchange—along with a few rentals—around the world, plus three supplements. Participants make direct contact. The cost is $65 for an annual subscription to the three directories and supplements, including a listing in one of the directories. Additional listings are $10 each, and an accompanying photograph costs $15. For more information, write VEC, P.O. Box 6550, Key West, FL 33041; or call 800-638-3841.

WORLDWIDE HOME EXCHANGE CLUB publishes two directories of homes for exchange around the world. Participants make direct contact. The cost is $29 for an annual subscription to the two directories, including a listing in one. Photos cost an additional $7. For more information, write WHE, 806 Brantford Avenue, Silver Spring, MD 20904; or call 301-680-8950.

WORLD-WIDE HOME RENTAL GUIDE publishes two catalogs of rentals each year. A subscription is $18 for one year, $30 for two years, $42 for three years. The cost to list a home begins at $150 and includes photographs. Participants make direct contact. For more information, write WWHRG, 3501 Indian School Road N.E., Albuquerque, NM 87106; or call 800-299-9886 or 505-255-4271.

INTERNSHIPS AND WORK PROGRAMS

AU PAIR HOMESTAY—USA & ABROAD places persons 18 to 30 years of age with families in France, Spain, Germany, the Netherlands, and Norway. Applicants must be at least a high school graduate, unmarried, and have child-care experience. Some countries also require language proficiency. Homestays last from three months to a year or more, and job requirements and pay vary. For more information, write AH, World Learning Inc., 1015 15th Street, N.W., Suite 750, Washington, DC 20005; or call 202-408-5380 or 412-681-5380.

LIVING POOR, by Thomsem, offers a clear-eyed look at what it's like to be in the Peace Corps. To order a copy, call or visit your local bookstore.

THE CENTER FOR INTERIM PROGRAMS matches applicants with one of more than 4,000 international travel, study, and work programs. Since 1978, its founder, Cornelius Bull, a former private-school headmaster with forty years' experience in education, has used his extensive network of personal contacts to find creative escapes for people of all ages. For more information, write CIP, P.O. Box 2347, Cambridge, MA 02238; or call 617-547-0980.

THE NATIONAL DIRECTORY OF INTERNSHIPS, edited by Sally Migliore, offers an annually updated list of internships, along with brief descriptions, available in the United States and some foreign countries. For more information, write to the National Society for Experiential Education, 3509 Haworth Drive, Suite 207, Raleigh, North Carolina 27609; or call 919-787-3263.

THE PEACE CORPS offers two-year paid programs in more than ninety countries. For more information, write PC, 1990 K Street,

N.W., Washington, DC 20526; or call 800-424-8580, extension 293.

WORLDWISE BOOKS offers helpful reference materials for people looking for jobs overseas. Its monthly newsletter, *International Employment Hotline*, lists job openings worldwide and reports on changes in the international job market. The cost for a one-year subscription is $39. Worldwise Books also publishes *How to Find An Overseas Job With the U.S. Government* ($28.95) and *International Internships and Volunteer Programs* ($18.95). For more information, write WB, P.O. Box 3030, Oakton, VA 22124; or call 703-620-1972.

Tips

• Don't limit yourself to formal internship programs. One of the best ways to find the internship you want is to propose it yourself to the employer or organization you're most interested in working for.

MAIL-FORWARDING SERVICES

Resources

MCCA INC., in business for more than twenty-four years, will forward mail and relay phone messages for about $13 per month. For more information, write MCCA, 1614 S.W. Seagull Way, Palm City, FL 34990; or call 800-478-9466.

TRAVELER'S OVERNIGHT MAIL ASSOCIATION charges a small monthly fee for collecting and forwarding your mail to you wherever you are traveling. For more information, write TOMA, Box 2010, Sparks, NV 89432; or call 702-331-1500.

TRAVELER'S REMAIL ASSOCIATION will accept your mail and forward it to you anywhere in the world for a monthly fee of about $13, plus postage; phone messages will also be relayed. Texas has no minimum residency requirement, an advantage if you want to avoid paying high state income taxes elsewhere (see Tips below). For more information, write TRA, 6110 Pleasant Ridge, Arlington, TX 76010; or call 817-478-9466.

Tips

• The post office will typically hold your mail for only one month, unless you seek special permission from the postmaster.

• If you are now paying state income tax or high vehicle taxes and you don't own a home, you may be able to use a mail-forwarding service to establish your permanent address in a less expensive state. Talk to your accountant or financial advisor.

MONEY

Resources

THE INTERNAL REVENUE SERVICE offers the "Tax Guide for U.S. Citizens Abroad," a free pamphlet on tax planning while abroad. For more information, write to the IRS office closest to you and ask for Publication 54; or call 800-829-3676.

UNION BANK OF SWITZERLAND offers a semiannual cost-of-living survey of major international cities. For a copy, send a first-class letter on letterhead to UBOS, 299 Park Avenue, New York, NY 10171; or call 212-821-4139.

Tips

• To find a qualified financial advisor near you, call the Institute of Certified Financial Planners, at 303-751-7600; the National Association of Personal Financial Planners, at 800-366-2732; or the Society of Independent Financial Advisors, at 303-850-9166.

SCHOOLS AND CULTURAL PROGRAMS FOR ADULTS

Resources

AMERISPAN offers language immersion programs, together with homestays, in countries throughout Central and South America. For more information, write AmeriSpan, P.O. Box 40513, Philadelphia, PA 19106; or call 800-879-6640.

ARTIST'S RESIDENCY PROGRAM, part of the historic Byrdcliffe Arts Colony, offers summer residencies lasting four to sixteen weeks to craftspeople, writers, and musicians, along with dance, film, video, theater, and visual artists. Private rooms and studio space are given when appropriate, and a living room, dining room, and kitchen are shared. The cost for a four-week session is about $500, and some scholarships are available to eligible applicants. For more information, write ARP, Woodstock Guild, 34 Tinker Street, Woodstock, NY 12498; or call 914-679-2079.

PETERSON'S publishes several helpful books for those interested in studying abroad, including information on financial aid and summer programs. For more information, write to Peterson's, P. O. Box 2123, Princeton, NJ 08543; or call 800-338-3282.

RAGDALE FOUNDATION, an Illinois artists' community established in 1976, offers twelve residents at a time use of the main house,

Barn house, and a studio. Room and board is $15 a day. Breakfast and lunch supplies are stocked in communal kitchens, and dinner is served six nights a week. Stays last from two weeks to two months, and writers, composers, visual artists, and artists of other disciplines are accepted. Special fellowships for Pan-African and older women writers are offered. For more information, write RF, 1260 North Green Bay Road, Lake Forest, Illinois 60045; or call 708-234-1063.

TRANSITIONS ABROAD, a bimonthly magazine, is chock-full of information on study, work, and travel opportunities abroad. Each issue focuses on a specific geographic area or theme. A one-year subscription is $19.95. Look for the magazine on your local newsstand or, for more information, write TA, 18 Holst Road, P.O. Box 344, Amherst, MA 01004.

SCHOOLS FOR CHILDREN

Resources

AMERICAN SCHOOL, a correspondence program for high-school age children, has enrolled more than 2 million students since 1897. Although the school is set up primarily for kids temporarily living away from home, it's also used by young tennis players on the professional circuit and child actors who can't attend regular classes. A large number of home-schooling parents also use the curriculum. Tuition is $379 a year, plus $100 for each subsequent year. For more information, write AS, 850 E. 58th Street, Chicago, IL 60637; or call 312-947-3300.

BEST OF K–12 INTERNET RESOURCES provides some of the best K–12 on-line resources available, including projects and lesson plans. Address: gopher://informns.k12.mn.us:70/11/best-k12

JON'S LIST OF HOME-SCHOOLING RESOURCES offers a list of on-line and community-based resources for home-schoolers. Address: http://www.armory.com/~jon/hs/HomeSchool.ht.ml

TEACH YOUR OWN, by John Holt, offers a good basic overview on how to teach your own children. For more information or to order, call Holt Associates, at 617-864-3100.

THE CALVERT SCHOOL advertises itself as "the school that comes to you," but it actually has two parts. One is a Baltimore day school with nearly 400 students from kindergarten through the eighth grade. The other is a correspondence school that has enrolled more than 350,000 students around the world since 1897. For approximately $400 a year, the school sends weekly packages containing instructions, lessons, books, and supplies to wherever you are in the world. It also provides a step-by-step instruction manual to teach parents how to teach their children. For more information, write TCS, 105 Tuscany Road, Baltimore, MD 21210-3098; or call 410-243-6030.

TRAVEL

Resources

APPALACHIAN TRAILWAY NEWS, published by the Appalachian Trail Conference, offers helpful information on hiking the Appalachian Trail. The newsletter is available only to members and the cost of membership ranges from $18 for students and seniors to $30 for families. To become a member, write ATC, P.O. Box 807, Harpers Ferry, WV 25425; or call 304-535-6331.

DISTANCE HIKER'S GAZETTE, published by the American Long Distance Hikers Association, Western States Chapter, provides information on hiking trails in the western United States, mainly the Pacific Crest Trail. For more information or to subscribe, write ALDHA-West, P. O. Box 804, LaPine, OR 97739.

EUROPE THROUGH THE BACK DOOR by Rick Steves and ASIA THROUGH THE BACK DOOR, by Rick Steves and Bob Effertz, offer lots of helpful pointers on how to travel well without spending a lot of money. Visit your local bookstore or, to order, call John Muir Publications, at 800-888-7504.

LEAGUE OF AMERICAN CYCLISTS has agreements with America West, Continental, Northwest, TWA, and USAir, allowing members' bicycles to fly free. Membership is $25. For more information, call 800-288-2453.

OCEAN VOYAGES INC. can place you aboard one of more than 300 yachts and charter sailboats in ports around the world. Novice sailors are welcome, and special interests can be accommodated. Most voyages range from one to eight weeks, but long-term stints—up to two years—are also available. For information, write OV, 1709 Bridgeway, Sausalito, CA 94965; or call 415-332-4681.

SERVAS INTERNATIONAL is a worldwide network of travelers and host families whose goal is to promote world peace through brief homestays with people of different backgrounds. Servas members share meals and accommodations with host families for a minimum of two days; lodging is free, and meals are usually provided free. The annual membership fee is $55. For more information, write United States Servas, 11 John Street, Suite 407, New York, NY 10038; or call 212-267-0252.

SPECIALTY TRAVEL INDEX spotlights 600 or so mostly small, unknown tour operators who feature offbeat opportunities, such as a chance to dig for dinosaur bones in western Colorado, bird-watch in South America, or tour Russia on horseback. For $10, you can order the adventure-specialty travel index guide for one year (two issues). For more information or to order, write STI, 305 San Anselmo Avenue, San Anselmo, CA 94960; or call 415-459-4900.

THE PACIFIC CREST TRAIL ASSOCIATION can answer many of your questions about hiking the trail. For more information, write PCTA at 1350 Castle Rock Road, Walnut Creek, CA 94598.

TRANSITIONS ABROAD (see entry above, under "Schools and Cultural Programs for Adults").

TWA AND BRITISH AIRWAYS both offer round-the-world ticket packages that allow you to circle the globe on one ticket. The fares are generally a bargain—$2,000 to $3,200—for an economy seat, but they carry some restrictions. Travel must be in one direction, for instance, and must be completed within one year. Most tickets also stipulate a minimum number of stops. Call British Airways (which offers a plan in conjunction with United Airways) at 800-247-9297 or TWA at 800-892-4141.

VOLUNTEER ORGANIZATIONS

Resources

PROJECT 67—ISRAEL offers kibbutz and moshav voluntary agricultural work in Israel. Volunteers age 18 to 35 work alongside the 2,000 permanent residents. Minimum work period is eight hours per day, six days per week, for eight weeks. Work packages allow for an open return ticket for travel after the stay. Costs range from $500 to $650. For more information, write Project 67—Israel, Hatton Garden, London, England, 8AH; or call 071-831-7626.

STAND UP AND BE COUNTED, by Judy Knipe, is a good general sourcebook on volunteering (Simon and Schuster).

VOLUNTEERS FOR PEACE INTERNATIONAL WORK CAMPS operates more than 1,000 community-service programs in fifty countries in Europe and Africa. For a $150 registration fee, volunteers live and work at a camp for two or three weeks—for example, at a camp responsible for the restoration and maintenance of a historic chateau in France—and many volunteers register for consecutive stays at different camps in order to spend several months abroad. For a free newsletter write to VPIWC, 43 Tiffany Road, Belmont, VT 05730, and state your country of interest. Or request the International Work Camp Directory listing over 800 projects. Published annually, it costs $12. For more information, call 802-259-2759.

VOLUNTEER VACATIONS, by Bill McMillon, is a concise, easy-to-read listing of more than 100 volunteer programs around the world. For example, you can canoe the Amazon and deliver medical supplies to the locals. An index lists programs according to price (most cost less than $500), project type, length of stay, and the season they're offered. For more information or to order, write VV, 2120 Green Hill Road, Sebastopol, CA 95472; or call 707-829-9364.

Index

Dear Reader,

Have you taken a great sabbatical that you'd like to tell others about? Do you have suggestions on other ways to plan, choose, or take time off? If so, we'd like to hear from you. You can E-mail us at SixMonOff@aol.com, or write us at:

Six Months Off
P.O. Box 2324
Portland, OR 97208